States of apology

MANCHESTER
1824
Manchester University Press

States of apology

Michael Cunningham

Manchester University Press
Manchester and New York
distributed in the United States exclusively
by Palgrave Macmillan

Published by Manchester University Press
Oxford Road, Manchester M13 9NR, UK
and Room 400, 175 Fifth Avenue, New York, NY 10010, USA
www.manchesteruniversitypress.co.uk

Distributed in the United States exclusively by
Palgrave Macmillan, 175 Fifth Avenue, New York,
NY 10010, USA

Distributed in Canada exclusively by
UBC Press, University of British Columbia, 2029 West Mall,
Vancouver, BC, Canada V6T 1Z2

British Library Cataloguing-in-Publication Data
A catalogue record for this book is available from the British Library

Library of Congress Cataloging-in-Publication Data applied for

ISBN 978 0 7190 8926 8 hardback

First published 2014

Edited and typeset
by Frances Hackeson Freelance Publishing Services, Brinscall, Lancs
Printed in Great Britain
by CPI Group (UK) Ltd, Croydon, CR0 4YY

Contents

Tables

Preface and acknowledgements

In 1999, I published a short article on the apology in politics.[1] At that time, there was relatively little written on the topic, however the years since have seen a large amount of work published in the area. This book is an attempt to consider the main issues raised by the apology in politics and to distil more than a decade's reflections on the topic. These reflections have been helped immeasurably by several people who have discussed ideas with me, organised seminars and conferences to explore these ideas further, provided references or other information and read drafts of articles and chapters. Principal among them are Pauline Anderson, Davide Denti, Tom Dickins, Graham Dodds, Cécile Hatier, Richard Kelly, Jan Löfström, Kevin Magill, Mihaela Mihai, Christopher Norton, Eamonn O'Kane, Debbie Orpin, Mathias Thaler and Simon Thompson. I would also like to acknowledge the School of Law, Social Sciences and Communications at the University of Wolverhampton for sabbatical support in the writing of this book and the *Journal of Political Ideologies* for permission to use material from an earlier article in Chapter 4.[2]

My two principal distractions from writing are walking and Crystal Palace FC. I would like to thank the aforementioned Messrs Dickins and Kelly, Duncan Cunningham and Steve Kibble for their companionship in the hills and Derek Miles for his company at the Palace matches. I would like to pay tribute to the diligence and support of the late Peter Mair as a supervisor, which helped to launch my academic career and, most of all, to thank Pauline Anderson for both her practical support concerning computers and her emotional support throughout this project.

Notes

1 M. Cunningham, 'Saying sorry: the politics of apology', *Political Quarterly*, 70:3 (1999), 285–93.

2 M. Cunningham, 'The ideological location of the apology', *Journal of Political Ideologies*, 16:1 (2011), 115–22.

Introduction

The apologies to be considered in this book are what I have termed political or state apologies and I will begin with a definition of these type of apologies. I use these terms to mean apologies made by state representatives or political leaders (e.g. presidents, prime ministers, chancellors) in their capacity as state representatives or political leaders and made on behalf of their states. Therefore, this would exclude, for example, apologies made for individual political misjudgements such as that by Nick Clegg, leader of the Liberal Democrats in the UK (see Chapter 3) and also apologies for transgressions in the personal sphere such as President Clinton's apologies for his activities in the Lewinsky affair.

The political or state apology has also been termed the official or national apology in some of the literature.[1] It needs to be distinguished from two other types of apology. The first type can be termed the institutional apology; those which are offered by non-state institutions such as religious and commercial organisations and NGOs. They share some of the characteristics of state apologies and some issues will be common to both, such as the question of collective responsibility and whether an organisation or institution can apologise for an event which preceded the existence of the members who currently constitute it. Clearly, there are also important differences between these types of apology as states have particular characteristics and responsibilities that set them apart from non-state actors. Two of these which are particularly pertinent to the apology are the relationship between state and citizen, and the state as an international actor and its relations with other states.

The second type of apology is the interpersonal apology. These typically occur between individuals as part of their private relationships. However, as Tavuchis has highlighted, they can take place between an individual and a group.[2] (For example, I could apologise for being late to a group of friends collectively hosting a party; this would be an interpersonal apology.) It should be emphasised that by using the terminology 'political apologies' for those made by states I am not claiming or implying that there are no politics involved in interpersonal apologies as I would subscribe to the view that there is a 'politics' in the broader use of the term within all personal, cultural and social interactions.

In reading the academic and journalistic literature relating to the institutional and state apology over a period of years, one is struck by two particular features of the phenomenon. First, the degree of consensus over the rise of the apology and the amount of apologies either requested or granted and second, the disparity in the evaluation of the worth of the apology. Therefore, I will begin by considering these features in a little more detail.

It is difficult to put a precise date on the rise of the apology. Nobles speaks of their emergence in the second half of the twentieth century while the majority view is that a significant increase occurred towards the end of that century. Celermajer dates the rise of the apology from the mid-1980s and Coicaud, in an article published in 2009, noted the 'special currency' of political apologies over the past twenty-five years. Lazare notes 'the rapid growth of apologies since the early 1990s'. Brooks and Thompson both note the rise of the apology without specifying its advent, although the examples given by Thompson date from the 1990s.[3]

Even if a precise date is hard to identify, it is clear that there is an increase in political apologies towards the end of the twentieth century. The following gives a flavour of authors' recordings of this development in order of publication. In 1999 Brooks argued that we had entered 'an Age of Apology' and in 2000 Barkan spoke of an 'avalanche of apology.' In 2001 Gibney and Roxstrom identified 'within just the past few years … a spate of state apologies' and Weyeneth in the same year noted that while not unique to modern times, 'we do seem to be witnessing a flurry of intense apologizing today'. In 2002, Thompson spoke of an 'epidemic of apology' and in the same year Govier and Verwoerd noted that 'several commentators' had employed the phrase 'the Age of Apology'.[4] These examples could be replicated; however this sample is sufficient to demonstrate that, by the turn of the century, it was accepted that there had been a large increase in apologies, particularly of the institutional and political variety.

The second phenomenon to be highlighted is the disjuncture between the academic and more 'popular' reception of this trend or development. As a generalisation, much of the academic work is supportive of the apology or at least its potential to achieve good ends.[5] It is seen as contributing towards, or potentially contributing towards, justice or reconciliation. It can have positive effects on relations between groups within the same polity or between different states and reflects a more generalised sensitivity towards the rights of minority groups or the legacy of past injustices.[6]

Despite this broad approbation, various commentators have drawn attention to the philosophical and practical complexities of the apology. For example, Tavuchis talks of the paradox of the apology in that it cannot undo what has been done and yet, in one sense, that is what potentially it can do if effective.[7] This may have a particular pertinence in inter-personal apologies in the restoration of relations yet could resonate in political apologies particularly between groups within the same polity. Lazare, in a discussion of Tavuchis, focuses on Tavuchis's implication that it is paradoxical that an apology is both, or can be both, complex and simple at the same time.[8] Also, as Coicaud among others has noted, there is the paradox, as he terms it, that the more heinous the injustice or offence, the more value the apology has yet it is the apology in this context that is often the hardest to offer and the hardest to accept. Consider the emblematic crime against humanity of the Holocaust. If the principal architects had survived, could an apology have had any meaning (however we understand that term) and could the survivors have ever accepted it? This is a hypothetical question but does point to what some have seen as both the necessity and impossibility of the apology.[9]

Although the apology throws up these philosophical and practical questions, it is the case that most academic writing sees value in the apology. However, the popular reception seems less favourable. There are numerous 'op. ed.' columns and journalistic pieces criticising or satirising the trend and this reached its apogee in the form of a novel, *The Apologist* by Jay Rayner published in 2004.[10] The basis for these critical and satirical stances is varied. Some of the criticism is based on the belief that politicians apologise to 'get themselves off the hook' and avoid further censure for transgressions and misdemeanours. However these examples would fall outside the definition of the state apology given above, because they are not offered on behalf of the state. Other grounds of scepticism about the apology include that it is offered as a way of avoiding, or seeking to avoid, other forms of reparation or restitution which have greater resource implications or that the apology, or some apologies, are incoherent or meaningless in that the politician making them was not responsible for the injustice and/or the recipients are not the victims of the injustice.[11] This latter point was summed up by the objection made by a Californian citizen to a proposed apology by the US government to current Native Americans for the treatment of their predecessors: 'you're asking people who didn't do wrong to apologize to people who weren't the actual victims'.[12]

It is difficult to account definitively for this disparity in attitudes. It may be that most of those academics who write about apologies are convinced by the intellectual and philosophical coherence of the phenomenon and that they tend to be more politically liberal than the journalists and commentators who are more dismissive of them. As defenders of the apology have pointed out, the fact that apologies may be used by individuals (or individual politicians) in a cynical manner does not mean that all apologies are cynical and should thus be dismissed.

The next section will provide a brief overview of 'where we are now' in the study of the apology. The texts cited above about the rise of the apology came from the turn of the twenty-first century and this marked the advent of an increase in literature about the political apology. Prior to this date, little was published with the large collection of case studies edited by Brooks in 1999 marking the start of a surge of material.[13] The vast majority of monographs and articles devoted to the apology date from 2000 and after.[14] These include works from the disciplines of, or influenced by the disciplines of, philosophy, political theory, theology, psychology, sociolinguistics, sociology, law and human rights. Other disciplines to which apologies would appear to have relevance but have received relatively little attention to date are those of conflict resolution and international relations (IR). The majority of general texts in these two disciplines have little or no consideration of the apology.

It would not be possible to provide a complete record of the topics covered by this literature. However a select list of the areas addressed includes what may be termed the definitional, the normative and the empirical. The first group covers those works which seek to define the apology, develop taxonomies and consider the connection between the personal and 'political' apology. The second group tends to make normative defences of the apology or consider its relationship to justice, forgiveness, repentance, reparation, etc. The third group considers in detail, for example, the genesis, reception, and impact of specific apologies through case studies.[15] It should be noted that much of the literature combines elements of the definitional, the normative and the empirical. As discussed in Chapter 1, a recent trend appears to be a focus on the diversity of possible forms and constructions the apology might take rather than the search for the definitive apology.[16]

The purpose and structure of the book

The purpose of this book is to provide an overview of what I take to be the principal issues in the consideration of the political apology and to suggest some ways forward in the study of the topic. Three disclaimers should be provided here. First, the book is aimed at the general reader who has an interest in the apology and thus avoids specialised and arcane language as far as possible while drawing necessarily on some political concepts and terminology for elucidation and illustration. Second, the text does not contain extended case studies. Specific examples are used to illustrate general points that, it is judged, do not need extensive case study detail. The bibliographical note provides details of further reading for those readers wanting more information about the case studies. Third, the sources used are English language ones, even though not all the examples focus on Anglophone countries. Therefore, some caution needs to be exercised in claiming the global relevance of the examples. As some commentators have pointed out, the phenomenon of the apology seems to be a global one yet more work needs to be done on the cultural understandings and meanings of the apology in different nations.[17]

Reflecting themes introduced above, Chapter 1 considers the relationship between the interpersonal apology, a long-established topic of sociolinguistic enquiry, and the state or political apology and considers taxonomies of apology. Chapter 2 focuses upon the explanations for the emergence of the political apology from approximately the mid-1980s. Chapters 3 and 4 respectively consider the philosophical questions and challenges relating to the apology and its location within dominant Western ideological traditions. Drawing on some of the themes of Chapters 3 and 4, Chapter 5 considers the politics of support and opposition in the intra-state apology while Chapter 6 focuses on the inter-state apology and the relationship between the apology and international relations theory. Finally, Chapter 7 examines the advantages and disadvantages of the political apology and attempts to assess its actual benefits.

Notes

1 Celermajer uses the term 'political' apologies in D. Celermajer, *The Sins of the Nation and the Ritual of Apologies* (Cambridge: Cambridge University Press, 2009). Nobles uses the term 'official' apologies in M. Nobles, *The Politics of Official Apologies* (Cambridge: Cambridge University Press, 2008) and Weiner uses the term 'national' apologies in B. Weiner, *Sins of the Parents: The Politics of National Apologies in the United States* (Philadelphia, PA: Temple University Press, 2005).

2 N. Tavuchis, *Mea Culpa: A Sociology of Apology and Reconciliation* (Stanford, CA: Stanford University Press, 1991).

3 Nobles, *The Politics of Official Apologies*, p. 4; Celermajer, *The Sins of the Nation*, p. 2; J.-M. Coicaud, 'Apology: a small yet important part of justice', *Japanese Journal of Political Science*, 10:1 (2009), 93–124, p. 96; A. Lazare, *On Apology* (Oxford: Oxford University Press, 2004), p. 251; R. L. Brooks, 'The Age of Apology', 3–11 in R. L. Brooks (ed.), *When Sorry Isn't Enough: The Controversy over Apologies and Reparations for Human Injustice* (New York: New York University Press, 1999), p. 3; J. Thompson, *Taking Responsibility for the Past: Reparation and Historical Injustice* (Cambridge: Polity Press, 2002), p. viii.

4 Brooks, 'The Age of Apology' p. 3; E. Barkan, *The Guilt of Nations: Restitution and Negotiating Historical Injustices* (New York: Norton, 2000), p. xvi; M. Gibney and E. Roxstrom, 'The status of state apologies', *Human Rights Quarterly*, 23:4 (2001), 911–39, p. 911; R. R. Weyeneth, 'The power of apology and the process of historical

reconciliation', *The Public Historian*, 23:3 (2001), 9–38, p. 36; Thompson, *Taking Responsibility for the Past,* p. viii; T. Govier and W. Verwoerd, 'Taking wrongs seriously: a qualified defence of public apologies', *Saskatchewan Law Review*, 65 (2002), 139–62, p. 139.

5 An example of an exception is Trouillot who argues that the lack of identity or coincidence between the apologising group and the perpetrators of the injustice can undermine the impact of the apology. See M.-R. Trouillot, 'Abortive rituals: historical apologies in the global era', *Interventions*, 2:2 (2000), 171–86.

6 Claims for the impact and benefits of the apology are considered further in Chapter 7.

7 Tavuchis, *Mea Culpa*, p. 5.

8 Lazare, *On Apology*, p. 23.

9 Coicaud, 'Apology', pp. 100–3. Coicaud also considers the concept of time and the relationship of the law to the apology in a section on the paradoxes of apology; however these do not seem to me to be paradoxes.

10 For a discussion of Rayner see N. Smith, *I Was Wrong: The Meanings of Apologies* (Cambridge: Cambridge University Press, 2008) and M. Marrus, 'Official apologies and the quest for historical justice', Occasional Paper No. 111 (Munk Centre for International Studies, University of Toronto, 2006).

11 These issues are discussed further in Chapter 3.

12 Cited in Weyeneth, 'The power of apology and the process of historical reconciliation', p. 25.

13 Brooks (ed.), *When Sorry Isn't Enough.*

14 The dates of bibliography entries that are dedicated to the apology support this claim. The impact of the apology has gone beyond the written text; the theme of Lebanese artist Rabin Mroué's *I the undersigned*, a two-channel monitor screening (2006) is the public apology.

15 Intra-state apologies (or the lack of them) to indigenous peoples and the state apologies of Japan and Germany are particularly well served by case studies.

16 See, in particular, Smith, *I Was Wrong.*

17 A. D. Renteln, 'Apologies: A Cross-cultural Analysis', 61–76 in M. Gibney, R. Howard-Hassmann, J.-M. Coicaud and N. Steiner (eds), *The Age of Apology: Facing up to the Past* (Philadelphia, PA: University of Pennsylvania Press, 2008).

1

The apology: definitional issues

The purpose of this chapter is threefold. The first purpose is to consider some understandings and ideas about what constitutes an apology in the personal sphere. This is necessary because the literature concerning the apology in politics or the state apology has generally used this as a starting point for comparison when considering what constitutes an apology in the sphere of politics. The second purpose is to review the discussion concerning what a political apology looks like and the third is to develop a typology of apologies by states which will help to inform the themes and discussion of subsequent chapters. There is no simple answer to the question 'What is an apology?' With this in mind, the first section will give examples of what different disciplines have considered to be the important characteristics of an apology.

Sociolinguistics and pragmatics are the disciplines which have the longest pedigree in the study of the apology; a study that can be traced back to the work of Austin in the early 1960s and Searle later that decade who were interested in the social and cultural context of language meaning and language use.[1] The apology is an example of what they termed a 'speech act'; a speech act being a statement or group of words that also constitute the performance of the act. One aspect of the speech act is that of illocution which relates to the act being performed, in this case the apology, and the act will employ a particular word or words which constitute what is termed the 'illocutionary force indicating device' (IFID).

The apology is a classic example of a speech act and central to the topic of politeness strategies, and thus in recent decades has become one of the most frequently researched topics in sociolinguistics and related disciplines.[2] Many taxonomies have been produced, however in their summary of developments in the discipline Harris *et al.* have identified five components of the apology which are common to much of the literature. These are an IFID token (e.g. 'sorry' or 'apologise'), an expression which indicates acceptance of responsibility or blame, an explanation or account, an offer of reparation and a promise of future forbearance. However these five components or criteria are not of equal weight as Harris *et al.* argue that the first two tend to be found generally in apologies while the last three tend to be more context- or situation-specific.[3] This is an important point because a theme of this chapter will be that while 'ideal type' apologies, interpersonal or in the public sphere, may be constructed and identified, many commentators argue that apologies which fall short of the ideal type may be effective or of value. This question will be addressed later in this chapter after a consideration of the more common features of the apology.

Three other examples will be offered, from the disciplines of philosophy, sociology and psychology. In an article written in 2000, Kathleen Gill claimed that philosophy as a discipline had largely neglected a consideration of the apology.[4] In an attempt at remedy, Gill offers five elements which comprise the fullest apology. These are that at least one party believes that the incident actually occurred, at least one party believes the act was inappropriate, someone is responsible for the act, the apologiser should have feelings of regret and remorse and the recipient is justified in believing the apologiser will refrain from such action again. It is interesting to note that Gill does not argue that all of these have to be explicit, especially in the case of minor infractions, but the fullest apology would include these elements or characteristics.

A decade before Gill's article, Tavuchis had published his oft-cited sociological study of the apology.[5] In an interesting parallel with Gill, he noted how little attention had been paid to the topic by his discipline. With respect to the interpersonal apology, Tavuchis drew on the established ideas of the apology as speech act with the aim of repairing relations between individuals. The minimal requirement of the apology was that one had to be sorry and to say so. He goes on to say: 'other features, for example, offers of reparation, self-castigation, shame, embarrassment, or promises to reform, may accompany an apology, but they are inessential because … they are implicit in the state of "being sorry."'[6]

This construction of an apology is largely replicated in the 2004 work of the psychologist Aaron Lazare. He offers the following definition of the apology. It 'refers to an encounter between two parties in which one party, the offender, acknowledges responsibility for an offense or grievance and expresses regret or remorse to a second party, the aggrieved'.[7] He later argues that the process of apology can be divided into four parts '1) the acknowledgment of the offense; 2) the explanation; 3) various attitudes and behaviors including remorse, shame, humility and sincerity; and 4) reparations.'[8] Lazare then emphasises the importance of context and situation in that not all of these four parts may be necessary in any given and negotiated apology. Thus a common theme that is emerging from texts from four different disciplines is that there are minimal requirements for an apology to 'count'; however the 'best' or fullest apology may have more features than the minimal criteria.

Before returning to a consideration of the interpersonal apology, it is worth a note here concerning Tavuchis's contribution to the debate which is relevant to the political apology. Although much of the text is concerned with the 'One to One' apology (the interpersonal), Tavuchis develops a four-fold typology of apology; the One to One, from the One to the Many, from the Many to the One and from the Many to the Many. The most important distinction between them is that the feeling of sorrow central to the interpersonal apology need not be a feature of the apology involving collectives; the most important feature of these apologies is that they are put on record. While an interpersonal apology can be rendered and be effective through 'ephemeral words', in the case of collective apologies 'the record, as idea and actuality, determines the preparation and formulation of the apology. This is where we can understand the speech itself; that it appears on public record *is* the apologetic fact.'[9]

It is worth noting that while Tavuchis argues that sorrow is not relevant to the apologies of collectives, such as corporations, the possibility of its pertinence in state apologies is less clear-cut. Some inter-state apologies are discussed in the section on Many to Many apologies which implies that sorrow and emotional engagement is likely to be absent. However, he does concede that the expression of sorrow by a nation as a collective would not strike us as unreasonable personification and therefore it is a meaningful idea.[10]

The interpersonal apology will be further discussed here, given its status historically as the 'backdrop' or context for discussion of the political apology. Given that we are all familiar with this type of apology, it may be useful here to map some of the above criteria or characteristics against a hypothetical example as beloved of philosophers. This will help to see if these analyses match a more intuitive or 'everyday' understanding of the apology and also the extent to which it can be undermined if these aspects are absent. Suppose I stay drinking in the pub and I am late home for dinner cooked by my partner. An apology would be in order because we both agree the incident happened and I accept that it was inappropriate; in this case it breached our implicit or explicit standards of consideration. The question of responsibility seems quite straightforward; I chose to stay drinking. However, for example, if customers were not allowed to leave the pub because the police wanted to interview potential witnesses to an incident this could reasonably be considered a mitigating factor. Mitigation may be more complicated than this. For example, if I chose to stay drinking because I ran into an old friend I had not seen for twenty years who was emigrating the next day, my partner might be less annoyed than if my drinking companion were a colleague I saw every day.

What would now constitute an apology or what action should I take? As indicated in the characteristics or criteria above, elements may be contingent and negotiable. An expression of regret may be sufficient or, as an indication of regret, reparation in the form of a bunch of flowers or box of chocolates. The point here is that between individuals what is an adequate or meaningful apology will generally be an issue for negotiation and no one template fits all occasions or applies to all individuals, or will necessarily be applicable across cultures.

It is fairly easy to identify factors that can undermine the efficacy of the interpersonal apology. In the example above, the lack of an IFID, the refusal to use the word 'apologise' or 'sorry' may be a problem. A frequent way in which apologies, both interpersonal and public, are undermined is through verbal constructions of mitigation, extenuation, evasion, and use of the passive voice. This could be crudely expressed as 'I'm sorry, but … ' when the apologiser provides various qualifications to the apology that, for the recipient, are likely to lessen its impact or bring into question its sincerity. The other factor common to the characteristics outlined by Gill, Harris *et al.* and implicit in Tavuchis, is that of forbearance. If I am late home from the pub for dinner on a weekly basis, my apology is likely to sound hollow and any undertaking not to repeat the action will be insincere and spurious.

The next section considers what issues arise as the apology becomes increasingly common in the public sphere. One result of this development is that the apology becomes analysed more by scholars in the disciplines of political theory, political science, sociology and theology as the topic moves beyond the sphere of the personal and interpersonal.

Two main topics need to be considered in light of this development; one is whether the components and characteristics of a political (or state) apology can be identified and the other is the ways in which this form of the apology differs from the more 'traditional' form of the interpersonal apology. It is possible that they may appear to be different beasts yet comparisons are made, implicitly and explicitly, because the same term is used for both.

Before this is undertaken, a cautionary note needs to be posted. It does not seem to me that an apology which the literature variously terms exemplary, formal, valid or coherent is necessarily a successful one. For example, it is plausible that an apology could meet a stringent list of criteria advocated by academics and political practitioners and be rejected by the intended recipients because they are unreasonable or have, for example, no interest in forgiveness or reconciliation. Conversely, an apology which fails to meet any particular set of criteria may be deemed successful if it leads to improved relations between the apologiser and those to whom the apology is made. This, I think, relates to the gap between empirical, 'messy' politics and the construction of ideal types. A 'successful' apology may not be a 'good' one and the estimation of the success of any actual, concrete apology may be difficult to gauge since its objectives may not be explicit or may be multiple or conflicting. This is why some authors, including Barkan and Karn and Weiner, have stressed that context and circumstance are important in the assessment of the form of the apology to be employed and the likelihood of success.[11]

Marrus, writing in 2006, also stressed the need to consider context, but argued that there was a large degree of consensus among students of the official (i.e. those issued by public bodies) apology about what constituted its formal elements. The four highlighted were: acknowledgement of a wrong committed, an acceptance of responsibility, an expression of regret or remorse for the harm done and the wrong committed and a commitment to reparation and, when appropriate (part of the fourth feature), to non-repetition of the wrong.[12] A similar list was provided by James in 2008 who outlines eight criteria for what he terms an 'authentic political apology'.[13] The apology: '1) is recorded officially in writing; 2) names the wrongs in question; 3) accepts responsibility; 4) states regret; 5) promises nonrepetition; 6) does not demand forgiveness; 7) is not hypocritical or arbitrary; and 8) undertakes – through measures of publicity, ceremony, and concrete reparation – both to engage morally those in whose name apology is made and to assure the wronged group that the apology is sincere.'[14] These criteria allow James to compare various state apologies and to judge some more robust than others.

The following section will attempt to explore a little more those elements that have been considered necessary or desirable for a state apology. These elements can be divided into four categories, termed the performative, the personnel, the language and the 'follow-up'. These terms may be a little clumsy but they capture the salient elements of most of the models of apology that have been developed.

Performative

By performative is meant any or all of the public elements of the 'acting out' of the apology. This can be significant for several reasons. First, in presenting the apology in a formal and/or ceremonial setting, the government or the official charged with the responsibility underlines and reinforces the importance of the apology. Second, the more 'high profile' the apology, the more likely it is to be on public record, the more likely the undertakings of the apologiser will be recorded and the more likely there will be a significant audience for these records.[15] This, in turn, has two potential benefits. It may, though this cannot be guaranteed, prevent any future reneging on commitments by the apologiser because the commitments are on record and it may help to reconcile and satisfy those to whom the apology is made because of the import and gravity of the occasion. Third, as well as emphasising the importance of the apology, the performative aspect may be the culmination, or part of the process, of the demos being involved in the consideration of the apology (especially for apologies to groups within the polity). For example, Celermajer has argued that the apology, or particular apologies, are informed by, and are a contemporary embodiment of, the act of collective repentance embedded in the Judeo-Christian tradition.[16] If this is the case, then the ceremonial and the public aspects of the apology are potentially very important.

The ritualistic element of the apology, and a critique of the tendency of academic study to focus on the verbal formulations to the neglect of 'dramaturgical ritual practices' is emphasised in the work of Horelt.[17] In light of Horelt's critique, it is plausible that the focus upon the linguistic or verbal aspects and components of the apology reflects the influence the disciplines of sociolinguistics and pragmatics have had on the subject.[18]

Personnel

The second element I have termed 'personnel'. This relates to the criterion found in many studies that the 'correct' person or people should make the apology and the 'correct' person or people should be the recipients. Who these people are may be subject to negotiation or may be a matter of dispute and the significance of this issue may be contingent or context-specific. The basic idea is that the person making the apology must have the authority or status to do so and, in the context of the state apology which is under discussion here, must be a recognised representative of the state. If he or she is not, the impact of the apology may be reduced or it may be considered invalid. Two examples illustrate this point. In the late 1990s, some of the campaigners seeking an apology from the Japanese for the treatment of allied prisoners of war and civilian internees in the Second World War argued that the apology should come from the Emperor because he was Head of State and was venerated in Japanese society. Therefore, they believed that resolutions of apology passed in the Diet by Japanese politicians did not constitute an adequate apology.[19] In 2000, a statement of regret about the discriminatory policies of the Bureau of Indian Affairs in the USA was made by an administrator, who was himself a Native American. According to Celermajer, the fact that the statement was not made by a member of the United States' executive undermined its impact.[20] In some cases, the impact of the apology is lessened, or it is considered inadequate, if delivered by someone whose status is inappropriate.

Relatedly, the apology should, ideally, be made to those who suffered the injustice or wrong under consideration. In the interpersonal example presented above, this is uncontentious since the wrongged party is easy to identify. However, with the official or political apology this is often a much more complex issue. There are three forms this complexity may take. First, those who suffered the injustice, or their representatives, may be divided about the necessity of the apology or the form it should take. There may be factionalism within the wronged party or among their representatives. Obviously, we cannot assume in politics that issues surrounding the legitimate representation of group interests are simple and that there will be unanimity within a particular group about who 'speaks' for it. This issue may be exacerbated if the role of spokesperson or representative brings significant material or status rewards. Second, as many political apologies involve long-past events, it is frequently the case that those who suffered the injustice first-hand are dead. Third, in some cases of apology, it is far from clear who comprises the wronged party or who can be considered to have suffered an injustice. These are questions and issues that will be considered in greater detail in Chapter 3.

Language

The third element under consideration concerns the use of language. As indicated already in this chapter, this has been a major issue in most of the work on apology because of the legacy of the disciplines of sociolinguistics and pragmatics. Again, which terms constitute an apology may be context-specific and cross-cultural factors may be important. It is banal to note that language and meanings are not fixed and immutable, therefore what constitutes an apology may be contested. However, if there is a perception by the recipients or observers that an IFID is absent or lacking this may undermine the apology. Much of the popular scepticism about the value of the apology, particularly relating to those given by certain commercial and religious organisations, is related to the lack of specific IFIDs indicating remorse or responsibility. As with interpersonal apologies, linguistic formulations involving mitigation, qualification, partial accounts or the use of the passive voice tend to undermine the value of the apology. In public apologies, which may involve individuals or groups, Lazare notes eight categories of failing which can undermine the proper acknowledgement of the wrong done and six of these relate to the inadequacy of the linguistic formulation.[21] To take just one classic and oft-cited example, the construction 'I'm sorry if you were offended' implies that it is the wronged party's overdeveloped sensitivity rather than the offender's transgression which is the real issue at hand.

'Follow-up'

The fourth element is that of 'follow-up'. This term implies some chronological sequence; however the ideas associated with this could accompany, or even precede, the apology. What I am trying to capture in this element are the actions, policies and commitments which complement or reinforce the apology. As with other aspects of the apology, these are contingent and context-specific. Reparation or restitution may accompany or follow the apology; reparation can take many forms including financial compensation to individuals, policies of benefit to the group or collective such as forms of affirmative action, funding of improved education and employment opportunities or more symbolic forms such as the construction of memorials or museums relating to the wronged group's culture. By 'restitution' I mean a more specific action or policy to restore what has been taken; for example the return of lands expropriated from indigenous peoples. One commitment could take the form of a statement of forbearance similar to that which was discussed with respect to the interpersonal apology.

To summarise the above, it is argued that the bulk of work on what constitutes an apology, or what constitutes an 'ideal type' apology, considers factors or elements which can be included within the four categories which here are labelled the performative, the personnel, the language and the 'follow-up'. It is a rare discussion of the apology that does not consider these and the relationship between them and much of the literature has applied these empirically through the use of case studies. This 'ideal type' apology can be presented in tabular form as in Table 1.1.

1:1: Elements of an 'ideal type' apology

Element of apology	*Performative*	*Personnel*	*Language*	*'Follow-up'*
Characteristics (not definitive)	Apology enacted in formal/ ceremonial setting	Made by authoritative person(s) to representative group	Acceptance of responsibility; lack of mitigation/ extenuation	Reparation/ restitution; material or symbolic

Before concluding this section with some considerations concerning the difference between the interpersonal and the political apology and a brief review of the trends in the literature about the apology, a couple of discursive points will be made about whether we can always identify an apology and also whether the identification of the 'ideal type' is necessary or useful.

In respect of identification, another hypothetical example from the interpersonal sphere will help to illustrate this. If a stranger in a pub accidentally spilt my drink it is conceivable that he or she might apologise profusely but not offer to buy me another one. Alternatively he or she might be very taciturn, say nothing but buy me a replacement and put it on the table. In the first scenario, I might accept the apology as sincere or might possibly consider it insincere (and maybe not an apology) because of the lack of material reparation. In the second scenario, I might think the apology was implicit because of the reparation or possibly think there was no apology because of the lack of an IFID. The point of this example is to try to illustrate whether there are objective criteria for an apology here or does it simply depend on my interpretation? It should be noted that one feature that often occurs in interpersonal apologies, the attempt to repair relations, is absent here because there is no prior relationship to repair. In the latter case, if whether an apology occurred is largely subjective, could this also be a feature of collective and political apologies?[22] If so, then trying rigidly to define an apology as having definitive criteria may be a chimera.

The differences and disparities in the four elements outlined above in particular cases can be illustrated by a brief comparison of the apologies made by the then British Prime Minister Tony Blair in 1997 for the Famine in Ireland and the 2008 apology made by the then Australian Prime Minister Kevin Rudd to the indigenous people of Australia. The commonalities here are that both of these events are usually referred to as apologies, which suggests that they fulfilled some generally recognised criteria of the apology and that both can be considered largely successful. The intention of Blair was to indicate a sensitivity towards nationalist feeling in Ireland and to acknowledge the traumatic impact of the Famine on Irish society, which was well-received within the Irish Republic. Blair's statement can be interpreted, in part, as a political 'balancing act' since it occurred shortly after a speech he had given in Belfast aimed at reassuring Unionists in regard to their concerns over the trajectory of the Northern Ireland peace process. This apology must be viewed in the wider context of inter-state relations and ongoing cooperation to manage the Northern Ireland conflict.

Rudd's apology was the most explicit recognition to date of the history of the institutionalised discrimination against, and the continued disadvantage of, the indigenous people of Australia and was broadly welcomed by their representatives and may be judged a success by this criterion.[23] The point highlighted here is that both apologies may be considered as of value judged consequentially relating to their success yet they appear poles apart if measured against the four 'ideal type' elements outlined above. The performative element in Rudd's apology was pronounced; the apology occurred in parliament right at the start of his tenure as Prime Minister and the occasion was shown on big screens in public venues in various Australian cities. In comparison, Blair's was much more 'low key' with the apology being read by the actor Gabriel Byrne at an arts festival rather than being presented by Blair, which also overlaps with the element of the personnel outlined above. The issue of the recipient of the apology also highlights differences; Rudd's was specifically to the indigenous people of Australia while Negash argues that it was unclear whom Blair was addressing in the text delivered.[24] In relation to the issue of language, the third element, Rudd made repeated use of IFIDs. In their study of the linguistic features of the speech, Augoustinos, Hastie and Wright note that that 'we apologise' and 'we say sorry' are used, in total, five times in the first forty-three lines of the speech. This use of IFIDs, they argue, 'make it explicitly clear that this is a direct, unambiguous and unqualified apology'.[25]

By comparison, the statement by Blair was much less explicit in relation to responsibility and did not contain the IFIDs 'apologise' or 'sorry'. The text read: 'The famine was a defining event in the history of Ireland and of Britain. It has left deep scars. That one million people should have died in what was then part of the richest and most powerful nation in the world is something that still causes pain as we reflect upon it today. Those who governed in London at that time failed their people in standing by while a crop failure turned into a massive human tragedy. We must not forget such a dreadful event.'[26]

In relation to the 'follow up', Rudd talks of both building a more unified nation and the need for policies and actions to address indigenous Australians' disadvantage.[27] In contrast, little specific was mentioned in the speech by Blair. With the last point, it is harder to make direct comparisons because in contemporary Australia Rudd had a policy responsibility in relation to indigenous Australians whereas the British government has had no responsibility for domestic Irish policy, with the exception of Northern Ireland, since the early 1920s.

The point of the example is that while one apology may be more complete and, in some ways, 'better' than the other in relation to the four elements in the sections above, it is arguable that both were effective, although the success of a particular apology may often be hard to gauge definitively. This should perhaps caution one against being too prescriptive about what constitutes or comprises an apology. With this codicil, two more issues will be addressed. First, in what ways does the political apology differ from the interpersonal apology and second, can a minimum set of criteria be identified for the constitution of an apology?

There are two principal ways and one less clear-cut way in which political apologies, apologies by states, differ from interpersonal ones. First, since political apologies are made by representatives on behalf of citizens, peoples or nations and the representative is not normally directly responsible for the injustice or transgression committed, they are apologies 'by proxy', to use Negash's term.[28] It can be argued, therefore, that it is not necessary or reasonable for the apologiser personally to feel emotions such as guilt, remorse or regret although, as Thaler notes, he or she may do.[29] In the case of interpersonal apologies, one would normally and reasonably expect the transgressor to exhibit this emotional engagement. Second, the issue of forbearance tends to be much less significant, and often absent, in the sphere of the political apology. This is either because the injustice occurred in the distant past and there is no realistic chance of it recurring or because the state making the apology has radically changed (or, at least, in its own evaluation) and is distancing itself from a previous incarnation. If the USA were to make an apology for slavery, however formulated, it seems unlikely that it would undertake not to enslave African-Americans in the future since that would be implicit in the apology and such enslavement is presumably beyond any conceivable trajectory of future American politics. However, as noted above, forbearance is often crucial to the interpersonal apology as the undertaking 'not to do it again' is often an element in restoring relations between the parties and recurrence of the transgressing behaviour renders the apology hollow and insincere.

The less clear-cut issue is, it can be argued, that of language. Most interpersonal apologies will probably have a linguistic component and contain one or more IFIDs, yet it is plausible to imagine an action taken without words which is intended as an apology and/or interpreted as such, as with the example of the restored drink.[30] This seems generally unlikely for a political apology though, as noted above, Horelt has critiqued much of the literature concerning the apology for emphasising the linguistic and speech act element to the detriment of the performative and dramatic element.

If the importance of contingency and context is accepted for defining what constitutes an apology and if it is conceded that particular apologies that do not seem to match up to the ideal type can have value, is there anything left that defines, or is a constitutive part, of all apologies? It could be argued that there should be two minimum requirements; one that a political apology should be public enough that there is some record and event that allows the polity and those affected to acknowledge, accept or critique it; it should not be 'smuggled out' or appear as a footnote, an incidental or an afterthought of the state's affairs. A second requirement is that some acceptance of responsibility must be present since it does not make sense to apologise for things for which one was not responsible.[31]

An important addition to the thinking about apologies has been provided by Smith in the 2008 text *I Was Wrong: The Meanings of Apologies* in which he argues against the idea that there is one sort of apology or that certain speech acts are either categorically apologies or not apologies.[32] He is interested in the social meaning of apology and this cannot be reduced to one single type. Smith details a variety of apologies all of which can be considered 'valid' as used in different contexts. For example, the most painstaking he terms the 'categorical' which are ethical acts which resonate with conceptions of repentance within religious traditions and thus resemble the type discussed by

Celermajer while other 'non-categorical' apologies demand less of the apologiser and may be much more instrumental. Smith's work takes further the idea that we can meaningfully talk of apologies rather than 'the apology', that different ones can be valid in different contexts and that IFIDs are not central to the way we should think about apologies.

The final aim of this chapter is to provide a four-fold typology of state apologies which will help to illuminate some of the themes considered in later chapters. This is important because some issues and critiques that relate and apply to one type of apology may be less pertinent or irrelevant to another. Intra-state apologies are defined as apologies by state actors to a particular grouping or community within that state. These can be subdivided into those relating to specific and fairly well-defined cases of injustice and those relating to more open-ended, continuous and extensive forms of injustice. Examples of the first type include the Tuskegee Syphilis Experiment in the USA and the internment of Japanese-Americans during the Second World War in the USA. Examples of the second type include the issue of slavery in the USA and the treatment of indigenous peoples in Australia and New Zealand. Inter-state apologies relate to relations between states and can be similarly classified into specific and well-defined injustices (type three) and general, extensive and continuous injustices (type four). Examples of type three are less common than the other types but could include the Katyn massacre of Polish troops by the Russian army in the Second World War and type four apologies include those relating to Franco-German relations and Japanese–Korean relations in the post-Second World War period.[33]

1:2: Typology of state apologies

	Specific	*'Open-ended'/continuous*
Intra-state	Type 1: Tuskegee Syphilis experiment; internment of Japanese-Americans	Type 2: Slavery in the USA; treatment of aboriginal peoples in Australia and New Zealand
Inter-state	Type 3: Katyn massacre	Type 4: Franco-German relations; Japanese–Korean relations

This chapter having reviewed and discussed the literature about what constitutes a political apology, the next chapter will explore some of the explanations of why it came to prominence from approximately the mid-1980s.

Notes

1 See J. L. Austin, *How To Do Things With Words* (Oxford: Clarendon Press, 1962) and J. Searle, *Speech Acts: An Essay in the Philosophy of Language* (Cambridge: Cambridge University Press, 1969). For a summary of speech acts, see J. L. Mey, *Pragmatics: An Introduction* (Oxford: Blackwell, 2nd edn, 2001), Chapter 5.
2 S. Harris, K. Grainger and L. Mullany, 'The pragmatics of political apologies', *Discourse and Society*, 17:6 (2006), 715–37, p. 716.
3 *Ibid.*, pp. 721–2. For a consideration of political apologies as speech acts see Celermajer, *The Sins of the Nation*, Chapter 2.
4 K. Gill, 'The moral functions of an apology', *The Philosophical Forum*, 31:1 (2000), 11–27, p. 12. In a review article MacLachlan noted that Smith claimed his 2008 book *I Was Wrong: The Meanings of Apologies* was the first philosophy monograph devoted to the apology since the twelfth century. (A. MacLachlan, 'The state of "sorry": official apologies and their absence', *Journal of Human Rights*, 9:3 (2010), 373–85.
5 Tavuchis, *Mea Culpa.*
6 *Ibid.*, p. 36.
7 Lazare, *On Apology*, p. 23.
8 *Ibid.*, p. 35.
9 Tavuchis, *Mea Culpa*, p. 102, emphasis in original.
10 *Ibid.*, p. 96. This will be considered further in Chapter 3.
11 E. Barkan and A. Karn, 'Group Apology as an Ethical Imperative', 3–30 in E. Barkan and A. Karn (eds), *Taking Wrongs Seriously: Apologies and Reconciliations* (Stanford, CA: Stanford University Press, 2006), p. 20; Weiner, *Sins of the Parents*, p. 24.
12 Marrus, 'Official Apologies and the quest for historical justice', p. 8.
13 M. James, 'Wrestling with the Past: Apologies, Quasi-Apologies, and Non-Apologies in Canada', 137–53 in Gibney *et al.* (eds), *The Age of Apology*, p. 139.
14 *Ibid.*
15 As noted earlier in this chapter, for Tavuchis the record is the essence of the collective apology.
16 Celermajer, *The Sins of the Nation.*
17 M.-A. Horelt, 'Public dramas of reconciliation: the ethnographic study of ceremonial and corporal elements in the deliverance of public atonement rituals in Katyn and East Timor' (Paper given at ECPR Conference, Reykjavik, 2011).
18 Weyeneth suggests that apology can be communicated in non-verbal ways ('The power of apology and the process of historical reconciliation', p. 20).
19 For more details of examples used and case studies cited, see the bibliographical note at the end of the book.
20 Celermajer, *The Sins of the Nation*, p. 32. Note, however, that Lazare has a much more positive reading of this speech (Lazare, *On Apology*, pp. 81–3).
21 *Ibid.*, pp. 85–106.
22 Willy Brandt's famous 'kneefall' in Warsaw in 1970 is commonly interpreted as a repentant and apologetic gesture which was committed without words. See also Chapter 6.

23 The phrase 'broadly welcomed' was used in one newspaper report. P. Smith, 'Rudd apology draws measured Aboriginal praise', *Financial Times* (13 February 2008), p. 8. See also the discussion in Chapter 5.

24 G. Negash, *Apologia Politica: States and their Apologies by Proxy* (Lanham, MD: Lexington, 2006), p. 10.

25 See M. Augoustinos, B. Hastie and M. Wright, 'Apologizing for historical injustice: emotion, truth and identity in political discourse', *Discourse and Society*, 22:5 (2011), 507–31, p. 515. For a critique of the opposition leader's statement, see B. Hastie, '"Excusing the inexcusable": justifying injustice in Nelson's Sorry speech', *Discourse and Society*, 20:6 (2009), 705–25.

26 Cited in M. Cunningham, 'Apologies in Irish politics: a commentary and critique', *Contemporary British History*, 18:4 (2004), 80–92, p. 82.

27 Augoustinos *et al.*, 'Apologizing for historical injustice', p. 527.

28 Negash, *Apologia Politica.*

29 M. Thaler, 'Just pretending: political apologies for historical injustice and vice's tribute to virtue', *Critical Review of International Social and Political Philosophy*, 15:3 (2012), 259–78, p. 266.

30 See also G. Pettigrove, 'Apology, reparations and the question of inherited guilt', *Public Affairs Quarterly*, 17:4 (2003), 319–48, pp. 324–5. Lazare provides examples of three non-verbal apologies (Lazare, *On Apology*, pp. 35–6).

31 The question of responsibility is considered in Chapter 3.

32 Smith, *I Was Wrong*. MacLachlan also emphasises the diversity of ideas about what constitutes an apology in the literature (MacLachlan, 'The state of "sorry"').

33 See the bibliographical note for a guide to further reading.

2

The emergence of the apology

Introduction

In the book's introduction it was noted that many commentators have remarked upon the upsurge in apologies, sought or granted, from approximately the middle of the 1980s. The consideration of the emergence of the apology throws up difficult questions of methodology, for example about the relationship between the material and the ideational in the emergence of particular political or intellectual trends; the apology having characteristics of both of these. Also, the question of the weighting of factors proves methodologically difficult in that it is easier to identify factors that contribute to the emergence of the apology than definitively to prove which are the most significant. This is perhaps best illustrated in a chapter by Fette, published in 2009, in which she lists some of the reasons put forward for the global emergence of the apology but does not comment further on their relative significance or the explanatory merit of them.[1] (She speaks of the reasons 'suggested' by scholars which could be interpreted to mean that there is not compelling evidence for some of these claims which may relate to the issue of methodological complexity indicated above.)

There are two other important cautionary notes to be posted relating to the emergence of the apology. It is plausible that different factors come into play in different types of apology. For example, the intellectual or political dynamics that inform intra-state apologies may be different from those that inform inter-state apologies, or effective political mobilisation for an apology may be easier to achieve with those apologies that are more contemporary than those long-distant. Also, one needs to be mindful of the salience of cultural difference which could render generalisations about intellectual and cultural shifts Anglophone-centric and thus be both politically insensitive and of limited explanatory value.

Bearing in mind these cautionary notes, it is possible to identify from the literature the factors which are pertinent to the emergence of the apology. First, there are those which can be termed the macro shifts in intellectual and cultural ideas. Second, are aspects of political change and development and, third, at the micro level, the influence of specific individuals as agents. In principle, it may be possible to trace the impact and salience of these factors in any empirical example of an apology though we cannot assume *a priori* all will be present in each case.

The purpose of this chapter is to examine the reasons why this upsurge took place. Although the focus of this book is the phenomenon of the apology, it needs to be emphasised that its emergence is best understood as part of a wider trend, politically and intellectually, of investigating the relationship between past and present. It is a fairly obvious point to make that the political apology is often about how the past is understood in the present and how the past is to be represented. However, the apology is only one manifestation of this disparate and cross-disciplinary phenomenon which includes, *inter alia*, issues of collective memory and trauma, the politics of commemoration and memorialisation, the politics of reparation and restitution, the debate over historical curricula in schools and the establishment of Truth and Reconciliation Commissions (TRCs).[2]

It may not be possible to generalise across all disciplines and all societies but to take one example, one can detect a broad trend in the discipline of history, or the Anglo-American practice of it, where the way in which history is remembered and the way memory finds contemporary representation became a focus of interest. Rather than 'telling the story' of powerful groups or, for labour and feminist historians who became more prominent in the 1960s and 1970s, 'telling the stories' of marginalised or neglected groups, interest developed among many historians in how these stories resonate in the contemporary period. In a sense, memory and representation can be seen as two key elements within this trend. It may not be conclusive evidence of this shift but it is interesting to note that a journal devoted to these connections, *History and Memory*, was first published in 1989, roughly contemporaneous with the rise of the apology and that, since the 1990s, such themes feature regularly in contemporary history journals.[3]

A useful way to locate and consider the rise of the apology is provided by John Torpey. In a study of the rise of reparations politics he identified four elements that constitute this wide-ranging phenomenon. Represented diagrammatically as concentric circles, he locates the various aspects of transitional justice as the 'core' and three other elements as other circles. In order of proximity to the core, these are what he terms compensation, financial and in-kind, apology/ regret and communicative history which includes issues of collective memory and physical memorialisation.[4] This indicates that the apology may be a part of the politics of reparations, or feature as part of an outcome of a Truth Commission but does not necessarily occur in all cases. It is worth noting here that some definitions of 'transitional justice' would be wider than Torpey's and tend to subsume all of his four aspects as part of transitional justice. A discussion of the broader topic of transitional justice is outside the scope of this work; however it is worth noting that it has become a massive area of study since the 1980s due to both the political changes that have facilitated it and, relatedly, the rise in an intellectual interest in the past and in memory. As Torpey states: '... we have witnessed the emergence of a veritable memory industry that preoccupies large numbers of academics and political activists'.[5] The appeal of transitional justice, broadly defined, intellectually and in the academy is that it is relevant to so many disciplines; a less-than-exhaustive list would include law, politics, political economy, development studies, sociology, history, psychology, theology and gender studies. An indication of the significance of the area is that at least four Anglophone academic publishers have series devoted to the topic and a dedicated journal *International Journal of Transitional Justice* was established in 2007.[6]

Macro shifts

The first of three macro shifts to be considered concerns the influence of universalism and human rights. The idea that people have certain rights as humans and that these are universal in the sense that everyone has them and the rights are, by definition, not culturally or temporally specific can be traced back at least to the European Enlightenment; therefore the shift is not the emergence of the universalist principle or paradigm. Rather, the shift relates to the experience of the Second World War, and in particular the Holocaust, giving new impetus to the need to recognise and to protect human rights.

The most immediate and significant institutionalisation of this trend was the creation of the United Nations (UN) and the adoption of the Declaration of Human Rights approved unanimously by members in December 1948. Subsequently the UN has ratified various Human Rights Conventions in areas which relate to various abuses that have featured in claims for apology. These include the Convention on the Prevention and Punishment of the Crime of Genocide (opened for ratification in 1948), the Supplementary Convention on the Abolition of Slavery, the Slave Trade, and Institutions and Practices Similar to Slavery (1956), the International Convention on the Elimination of All Forms of Racial Discrimination (1966), and the Convention Against Torture and Other Cruel, Inhuman or Degrading Treatment or Punishment (1984).[7]

Govier and Verwoerd are among the authors who argue that the rise of the apology is linked to a 'developing moral consensus' about human rights, an idea or set of ideas about universal standards of treatment which can be operationalised both within and between states.[8] Gibney and Roxstrom note that many apologies in the domestic sphere reflect established human rights' principles even if they are not articulated within such language and also that apologies between states can inform developments in international law or draw on clauses within it.[9] In addition to the UN conventions noted above, Gibney and Roxstrom and Bilder cite developments within the UN that more explicitly recognise the role of the apology. The UN Basic Principles and Guidelines on the Rights to a Remedy and Reparation for Gross Violations of International Human Rights Law and Serious Violations of International Humanitarian Law detail five categories of reparation. One of the five is termed 'satisfaction' of which public apologies are listed as one possible type along with, for example, commemoration and memorialisation.[10]

Relatedly, Torpey has examined the effect of the Holocaust and the defeat of Nazism on the politics of reparation of which, as discussed above, apology can be considered a part.[11] These are seminal events in the understanding of this form of politics for many reasons. These reasons include the move of the politics of racial superiority into the European theatre in such a starkly genocidal form, and its ultimate defeat. These developments meant that in the post-war period the politics of racial classification and discrimination were largely discredited. This did not mean, of course, that discrimination did not occur; however the defeat of Nazism and fascism provided marginalised groups the opportunity to try to articulate demands using the ideological backdrop of liberal conceptions of freedom and universalism which had been mobilised against Nazism and fascism. Also, as Holocaust survivors and their supporters mobilised for reparation, compensation or forms of memorialisation, the Holocaust became a template on which other groups articulated their claims and would try to engage 'Western' sympathy or support for such claims.[12] As Torpey puts it: 'the Holocaust has not only absorbed an enormous amount of attention among those wanting to come to terms with the past; it has also facilitated attention to the catastrophic past more generally'.[13]

The second political trend associated with the rise of the apology is what may be loosely termed 'identity politics'. This is the mobilisation of a group based on a shared identity which has been perceived to have been marginalised, discriminated against or not accorded recognition by the dominant culture within a particular polity. It should be noted at the outset that 'identity politics' is often underpinned and supported by an intellectual tradition which explicitly critiques the universalist, liberal narrative outlined above. This critique holds that universalist principles are not adequate in recognising and validating the cultures, norms, etc. of minority cultures and, in practice if not intention, privilege those of the majority. It is not only (openly) autocratic and undemocratic regimes that have failed to give recognition to minority cultures and sensibilities but also liberal-democratic regimes which do not recognise the limitations of their conceptualisations of justice and equality.

This intellectual and political development is particularly pertinent with respect to ethnically based identity politics. Many cases of intra-state apology are related to mobilisations by groups which have been historically discriminated against on the basis of ethnic identification, and whose contemporary position is informed by that discrimination.[14] Torpey makes the point that many claims for reparation, some of which include the apology, are related to the rise of 'greater ethnic self-assertion'.[15]

It is important to note that some of this critique may be about the practices of liberal democracies but is also rooted in a philosophical critique of the limits of liberalism. For example, Celermajer associates the rise of the apology, and specific apologies, with a response to the inadequacies of liberalism, as an ideology, to theorise or to emphasise adequately the contemporary presence of collective repentance which draws on pre-modern theological traditions. Liberalism also conceptualises justice and reparation in an individualistic and procedural fashion which fails to capture the collective nature of identity and responsibility.[16]

A slightly different way of thinking about the rise of regret, which may be linked to the apology, is provided by Olick. His analysis argues that the phenomenon does not represent the triumph of universalism or of a Hegelian 'world historical idea' but is rather a manifestation of historical and sociological currents in which pluralist perceptions and multiple histories have come to the fore.[17] In this account there are echoes of the postmodern idea that there is no one historical truth or narrative to be discovered or recorded but a series of conflicting and ultimately irreconcilable versions and the age of apology is, in part, about the challenging of elite versions of history by the marginalised.

If the broad explanatory frameworks of the post-war revival and application of liberal universalism and the emergence of more particularistic 'identity politics' are in philosophical tension, is the implication that one of these explanatory models relating to the apology is wrong? My response is that this is not the case for two reasons. First, political mobilisation is practical politics and those engaging in it with a view to securing an apology may employ a variety of strategies and discourses which draw on different intellectual traditions and use rhetoric or discourse that political philosophers or others may find inconsistent. Politicians and political activists are not obliged to choose between competing conceptualisations of, for example, responsibility or justice.

It may also be objected that the gap between liberal formulations and identity politics drawing on communitarian thought is not so vast. In trying to theorise restitution, Barkan identifies a 'neo-Enlightenment' tradition informing the contemporary practice in which a core of liberal principles is enveloped by social and cultural values which result from local traditions and preferences.[18] This resonates with ideas, particularly associated with Will Kymlicka, that liberal notions of citizenship and equality are compatible with specific policies designed for particular groupings within society with a view to preserving aspects of cultural heritage or a 'way of life'.[19]

Second, the previous chapter noted that many authors have emphasised the contingent or context-specific nature of political apologies. This implies a large variety of what constitutes an apology and it is likewise plausible that different apologies will be informed by different intellectual or philosophical traditions. Variables may include the type of hurt or injustice for which redress is sought, the composition of the group seeking it and the political orientation or ideology of the government from which an apology is demanded.

The third shift at what I have termed the macro level relates to cultural practices which several authors have linked to the practice of apology. In particular, this concerns developments by which Anglo-American culture has become increasingly confessional and performative. The following section will provide a flavour of what is meant by this and then some considerations on its relation to the political apology. It is difficult to date the advent of the phenomenon precisely but there seems broad agreement that recent years have seen a rise in public displays of emotion, including guilt, remorse, regret and shame. This can be contrasted with a popular perception, whether empirically grounded or not, that until relatively recently this did not occur and would have been frowned upon. In the British context at least, this reticence to show emotion may be captured in the popular phrases of 'the stiff upper lip' or 'getting on with it'. (There is some evidence that combatants in the Second World War and Holocaust survivors did not speak of their experience, particularly in the immediate aftermath of the events.)[20] Another example of this British reserve and stoicism which is cited both by Furedi and featured in Hislop's trilogy of documentaries about the history of emotion is the Aberfan disaster of 1966.[21] In South Wales, 116 children and twenty-eight adults died when a coal-mine spoil heap buried a school. Existing archive footage of TV news interviews with parents of trapped children reveals a stoicism and communal self-reliance which Furedi argues would not occur in contemporary Britain.

At a popular, and populist, level this more recent phenomenon of openness and emotional display is exhibited in the confessional TV programmes which encourage people to confess various transgressions to those wronged and, obviously, to have the confession witnessed by an audience. Here, the confessional and performative are united. In 2001, Cohen noted that 'on Oprah, Phil, Sally and Jerry, the act of confession and testimony is being perfected'; this being a reference to the popular American daytime confessional shows of Oprah Winfrey, Phil Donahue, Sally Jessy Raphael and Jerry Springer.[22] In 2003, Elshtain made disparaging reference to the same shows, arguing that their tawdry nature cheapened the concept and value of forgiveness.[23]

Torpey has also commented on the link. Interestingly, he draws links, while conceding the difference in seriousness, between the confessional of *The Jerry Springer Show* and the narrations of the South African Truth and Reconciliation Commission.[24] However he speaks of sensing at least a superficial connection which relates to a theme which will be pursued below; that of whether and how we can establish linkages between the political apology and the rise of the confessional culture.

Apart from the confessional TV programme, one can provide other examples of cultural practices in the last twenty years which suggest, if do not definitively prove, the occurrence of a cultural shift. In 1990, Paul Gascoigne cried publicly when sent off in a World Cup match and subsequently various sportspersons, including resigning England cricket captains, have cried at press conferences or at other public occasions. A recent example within a sporting context is the closing of the 2012 summer Olympics held in London. As part of its montage to mark the closing ceremony, the BBC showed clips of crying athletes. It was not possible to tell if they were crying from joy, pain or despair but that is beside the point. It is hard to imagine, if not inconceivable, that thirty or forty years ago there would be such public displays of emotion or that the BBC would have featured them so prominently.

These public displays of emotion are also reflected in the reaction to death and public mourning. In 1997 the death of Diana, Princess of Wales, resulted in a massive and prolonged display of public grief; such was the seeming unanimity and depth of feeling that one dissenting voice used the term 'floral fascism' to characterise the phenomenon.[25] Furedi sees this event as a watershed in the move from Britain's reputation for reticence and control: 'after the unprecedented display of public emotionalism over the death of Princess Diana … it is difficult to sustain the myth that Britain is the land of the stiff upper lip. Since this event, the powerful influence of therapeutic culture on British society has been widely acknowledged'.[26] Other examples relating to death include the practice of leaving floral or other tributes, such as toys or replica football shirts, at the scene of fatal accidents or violent deaths. In some of these cases, it seems, the donors of tributes had no personal relationship to the victim, as was the case with the overwhelming majority of mourners for Princess Diana. Similarly, in 2011, the death of Gary Speed, the Welsh football manager, was marked by applause in tribute at matches taking place at clubs with which he had no connection as player or manager.

The last example of the rise of the 'confessional culture' to be noted is the popularity of 'misery lit'; a term which refers to autobiographical works in which typically the author lays bare histories of various forms of abuse at the hands of parents, foster parents or institutions. This phenomenon dates from approximately the early 1990s with the best-selling memoir *A Child Called 'It'* by Dave Pelzer published in 1995 cited as the trend-setter, although the 1992 work *Wild Swans* by Jung Chang is sometimes considered an example of 'misery lit'. Three features of these books are worthy of note here. First, as with 'confessional' television, they originated in the USA and spread to the UK and Ireland and thus seem to be significant in, if not exclusive to, Anglo-American culture. Second, they proved very popular. In 2006, it was estimated that eleven of the 100 best-selling paperbacks were of the genre and comprised 8.8 per cent of paperback sales and by that date leading book retailers had specific sections devoted to these books.[27] Another indication of their popularity was that by 2004 Pelzer's *A Child Called 'It'* was in its thirty-fifth impression and the best-selling Limerick memoir by Frank McCourt, *Angela's Ashes* (1996) was adapted into a successful film. Third, these books proved controversial for two reasons and provoked something of a backlash. Many of the authors claimed that their motivation was catharsis or to help or be an inspiration to other 'survivors' of abuse; however, many critics felt that some readers were motivated by voyeurism, prurience or titillation.[28] Also, many of the books which were claimed to be factual were either somewhat economical with the truth or were works of fiction.[29]

There is an argument, then, that since approximately 1990 there has been a large increase in personal displays of public emotion and in the collective marking of loss or death. Commentators have been divided with some seeing these phenomena as representing a collective self-indulgence, mawkishness or sentimentality whereas others have interpreted them as a welcome development, indicative of Britain becoming a more empathetic or compassionate society.[30] However the issue here is not normatively to evaluate the phenomena but rather to explore their link to the politics of apology.

There are two issues that need to be considered here. The first is that the literature discussing the apology that draws attention to the more openly emotional and confessional nature of culture gives examples almost exclusively from the UK or the USA. However, much of the literature also notes that the phenomenon of the apology is a global one. What, then, is lacking is empirical evidence that there has been a cultural shift in other societies which somehow relates to the apology. Logically, it could be argued that the confessional culture which has emerged in Anglo-American society (and perhaps other Anglophone countries that are influenced by this culture) is related to the apology but also that the apology has gained traction in countries where such a cultural shift has not occurred.

The second issue is that the relationship between culture and politics is difficult to theorise and assess. There is good empirical evidence that the political apology became more prevalent in the UK from the 1990s and that this coincided with the rise of a more confessional culture. However, of course, this does not necessarily demonstrate any causal link between the two developments or how they might inform each other. That said, it is plausible to suggest that there may be some connection since what has been termed 'culture' here and politics do not exist in hermetically sealed worlds. For example, if British society has become more performative and one in which many citizens see public shows of emotion as either legitimate or laudable, politicians may make a calculation that the political apology (or particular forms of the apology) will be understood as an acceptable form of political practice and those groups with grievances may want a public or performative acknowledgement of these grievances reflecting such cultural shifts.

Political change and development

Having reviewed the emergence or revival of intellectual and cultural ideas which the literature has identified as providing discourses that those seeking apologies can employ, the second area to be considered is that of political change and opportunity. The world is full of potential apologies, or other forms of reparation, given that world history contains innumerable injustices. For these potential ones to be articulated or recognised there need to be propitious political circumstances.

The most important factor here is the process, or various processes, of democratisation. Two broad types of this process can be identified and distinguished: the transition of authoritarian states towards democracy and the extension of rights to members of polities which already claimed democratic status. Examples given of the first type typically include the processes in former Communist countries following the end of the Cold War and the collapse of the Soviet Union, the democratic trends within Latin and Central America following the replacement of right-wing authoritarian governments (for example, Chile, Argentina and Guatemala) and the transition of South Africa from the system of apartheid. The significance of these is indicated in that one commentator has employed a two-fold typology in which 'transitional apologies', those which closely follow regime change, are distinguished from 'historical apologies' which tend to deal with injustices from longer past.[31]

Many, though by no means all, of the 'transitional' processes have been accompanied by or utilised Truth and Reconciliation Commissions (TRCs) and, as noted above (see p. 22), Torpey has linked these and apologies together as part of the broader process of reparations politics. Therefore, it is worth making some observations about TRCs and their relationship to the apology.

Although she recognises there may be definitional issues about exactly what constitutes a TRC and that her list may not be exhaustive, in the 2001 edition of her book *Unspeakable Truths* Priscilla Hayner listed twenty-one TRCs, five of which she termed 'illustrative' and sixteen as 'less prominent'. The growth in TRCs is illustrated by the fact that in the second edition published in 2011, Hayner identified forty TRCs; five of which she studied in greater detail as the strongest and twenty of the others were examined as illustrative.[32]

Three points should be highlighted here. First, the chronology of the TRCs closely fits the rise of the apology identified in the introduction. Only one of the forty listed (that of Uganda) was established before 1982. Second, of the thirteen countries which Hayner selects in the second edition to try to assess the impact of TRCs, an apology features in eight of the cases.[33] As Hayner discusses, it is often difficult to assess precisely the impact of TRCs; however it may be tentatively suggested that while apologies appear in many cases they do not seem to be central to many countries' experience of transitional politics or justice. Third, TRCs, or at least as defined and considered by Hayner, are much more common in the non-communist transitions, particularly in Africa and South and Central America. Of the forty case-studies, only the former East Germany and Yugoslavia feature as post-communist transitions.[34]

The second form of democratisation typically involves countries that had long claimed democratic status yet had not extended full rights to members of the community. The treatment of indigenous peoples in Australia, New Zealand, the USA and Canada are examples that fall into this category. This democratisation is of a different order in that it does not mark part of a political transition but reflects the extension of democratic rights or recognition within existing states. As a generalisation, the apology, claimed or granted, appears more important in these cases, often fuelled by political mobilisation and the publicity given to previous and sometimes still-current abuses.[35]

It is obvious that not all liberal democracies apologise or that not all democracies apologise for all transgressions committed, yet democracy seems to be a background condition for apology. Empirically, it is democracies which apologise and non-democracies that do not and it is democracies which have the political culture and representational structures and mechanisms which potentially allow the mobilisation of groups to press for the apology. Clearly, the resources on which groups can draw for mobilisation are varied and will differ over time and between polities. One example will suffice here. A less than comprehensive list of the strategies and tactics used by a marginalised group (African-Americans) to gain civil rights in the 1960s includes variously rhetorical appeals to justice, equality and the immorality of discriminating on the basis of race, a rhetoric based on the development of 'identity politics', civil disobedience, economic boycotts, violence, alliances with white liberals, voter registration drives and attempts to have ruled unconstitutional the discriminatory practices of state governments.[36]

It may be noted here that those seeking an apology are often, if not always, a minority and may lack extensive material resources. This may, in some cases, make the use of normative rhetorical claims all the more important; for example by persuading the majority community that the apology, or other reparation, is just or fair in relation to universalist values or by persuading them that a specific culture and 'way of life' are worthy of respect as part of a 'thicker' idea of citizenship identity.

Individuals as agents

The third factor for consideration is the role of specific individuals in the realisation of the apology. Without the ideological developments and the political structures of democracy as 'background conditions' indicated above, it seems implausible that individual agents could successfully effect or realise the apology. However the role of particular politicians has been noted as making a difference in the literature. One might assume that politicians of the democratic 'left' might be more politically disposed to apologise than those of the 'right'; the former being more sensitive to minority concerns and the latter adopting a more 'hard nosed' realist attitude towards politics.[37] While there is some evidence for this, the position is a little more nuanced, as shown later in this chapter.

Examples where political inclination made a difference to the emergence or development of the apology include the roles of Murayama, Clinton, Blair and Rudd and these will be briefly considered. In 1995, the socialist Prime Minister of Japan, Murayama issued an apology to South Korea for Japan's wartime role which went beyond the more qualified ones of his predecessors.[38] US President Clinton was associated with a variety of apologies, or qualified forms thereof, which brought forth criticism from Republican opponents and the 'right' who interpreted his statements as manifestations of liberal weakness. While Blair, British Prime Minister from 1997 to 2007, engaged in fewer apologies, some commentators viewed the apology concerning the Irish Famine as symptomatic of a woolly liberalism informing parts of the New Labour project.[39] These perceptions of Clinton and Blair can be contrasted with those of recent conservative leaders of their respective countries, George Bush Sr and Margaret Thatcher whose forthright, unreflective nationalism made them unlikely sources of apology.[40] Writing in 2000, Barkan identified Blair and Clinton, along with President Chirac of France and Chancellor Schroeder of Germany as examples of leaders whose politics exhibited a degree of 'national self-reflexivity',[41] and Clinton and Blair were described by one journalist as the two men who 'probably inaugurated this era of politics with a human face'.[42]

The case of Kevin Rudd, Labour Prime Minister of Australia, is perhaps the best example of where the political inclinations of individual politicians have made a difference. In 2008, on entering office, Rudd made what is widely regarded as a successful and unqualified apology to the indigenous peoples of Australia. This contrasted starkly with his predecessor, John Howard, who earlier rejected the apology, viewing it as part of the 'black armband view of history'. Howard believed that an apology by contemporary Australians for past wrongs was politically unnecessary and philosophically incoherent.

Barkan's reference to the French President Chirac of the Gaullist centre-right who, in 1995, apologised for the anti-Semitic policies of the wartime Vichy government indicates that there is no simple left/right split here among politicians. Also, we cannot assume that a particular individual will be in favour of, or opposed to, apologies *per se*. This can be illustrated by a case study of the attitudes of the Conservative British Prime Minister, David Cameron.

In 2006, when leader of the opposition, David Cameron expressed his doubts about the value of an apology for Britain's role in the slave trade on the grounds of it being such a long time ago.[43] The context of this remark was discussion about how to mark, in the following year, the bicentenary of the abolition of trading slaves in British ships. In February 2013, on a visit to India, Cameron as Prime Minister expressed remorse but refused to apologise for the Amritsar massacre of 1919. This was an event when at least 379 Indians were killed by British soldiers during a nationalist demonstration, though some estimates put the death toll nearer to 1,000.[44] There were two reasons cited as to why Cameron did not offer an apology; one was that that the British state acknowledged the massacre at the time and established a formal inquiry which resulted in the commanding officer being removed from his position. Second, it was suggested that Cameron, or his officials, were concerned that an apology could set a precedent for other demands for apologies concerning events in Britain's imperial past. Two observations will be made here. First, the fact that a contemporary inquiry was held, which did not include an apology, does not preclude the making of an apology by Cameron.[45] Second, the concern about precedent is interesting given that Cameron holds a generally benign view of Britain's imperial past. In 2009, in the context of criticisms of colonialism by Blair and Brown, the former and current Labour Party leaders, he stated: 'we must never forget that Britain is a great country with a history we can be truly proud of'.[46] If Cameron's view is accurate, presumably there would be no grounds for the generation of numerous claims for apology. Another contributing factor in Cameron's position may have been that an apology in this context would not sit well with his MPs and Conservative Party members.

By contrast, in two other cases Cameron did issue an apology. In June 2010, he offered an apology for the killing of fourteen civilians by British troops in Londonderry, Northern Ireland, in 1972, an incident known as 'Bloody Sunday', and in September 2012 he apologised to the families of the victims of the Hillsborough disaster, in which ninety-six Liverpool supporters had been crushed to death at a football stadium in Sheffield in 1989. In both cases, the tone, gravity and presentation of the apology was widely considered impressive.[47]

Why, then, did Cameron believe an apology appropriate in the latter two cases? It can be argued that they had characteristics in common which did not pertain to the slavery case and the Amritsar massacre and these factors influenced Cameron's decision. The following characteristics can be identified. First, the injustices were comparatively recent. Second, these were incidents which had both been subject to initial reports or inquiries that were so inadequate or partisan that they amounted to 'cover ups'. Relatedly, the apologies followed closely upon the publications of reports which presented a mass of evidence showing that the original investigations and reporting of the incidents failed to present the truth. Third, Cameron was in office when the reports were made and so he accepted a responsibility which did not apply to the Amritsar massacre. Fourth, in the cases where Cameron apologised, the victims were UK citizens which meant that the Westminster government had a responsibility to, and for, them. (It is probable that many of those killed on 'Bloody Sunday' and their families would not have described, or do not describe, themselves as 'British'; however they did, or do, live in part of the UK and the point about political responsibility stands.) However, this is also the case with Amritsar although not with victims of slavery. In the Amritsar case, Cameron appears to believe that the responsibility of the British state was discharged with the inquiry and thus he is exempted from an apology. One additional point should be made here. A government source was cited as distinguishing the 'Bloody Sunday' apology and Hillsborough apologies from the Amritsar apology because, in the former two cases, 'the state, or organs of the state, were at fault' while at Amritsar it was the fault of an agent of the state, a reference to the officer Brigadier-General Dyer.[48] It is certainly debatable whether such a clear distinction can be made between Amritsar and 'Bloody Sunday'; this claim may have been circulated as an additional, if unconvincing, reason for Cameron's position.

One other factor to consider in the two apologies is the public reaction. Following the Hillsborough report of 2012, it seemed clear that the British media and public were largely supportive of the apology by Cameron for what he termed the 'double injustice' – the inadequate safety procedures and emergency service responses that caused the deaths and the subsequent attempt by the South Yorkshire police to attribute blame to the actions of the victims or other supporters. It might have been anticipated that the response to the 'Bloody Sunday' apology would be less unanimous. Factors such as the context of the IRA campaign and the perception that the massively prolonged and costly Saville Inquiry, which ran for twelve years and cost nearly £200m, was a sop to republicans who had been members of, or had close links to, the IRA could potentially reduce support for the apology.[49] However a subsequent public opinion poll indicated that about 60 per cent of British people and about 70 per cent of people within Northern Ireland approved of the apology.[50]

It is difficult to assess to what extent the public reaction or support was a factor in these apologies. It is plausible that Cameron believed that justice did require an apology in both cases and that the Hillsborough apology would be largely welcomed and that a favourable political reception of the 'Bloody Sunday' apology by the nationalist community in Northern Ireland balanced the more diffuse criticisms or reservations from the Unionist community there and from some of the British public.[51]

The chapter will conclude with a summary of reasons as to why the political apology became more prevalent and widespread in the last fifteen years of the twentieth century. The explanations can be broadly divided into those which focus on the emergence or strengthening of ideological frameworks that can be rhetorically invoked, those that emphasise the importance of democratisation and the democratic process and the opportunities for political mobilisation which this process provides and those which draw attention to the role of individual agents. It seems that it is probably impossible to assign precise weightings to these factors or to go beyond a claim that each concrete apology will contain an interaction between them.

An additional point here is that the emergence or increase in apology may have created its own momentum and a 'snowball' effect was established. The increase in forms of, and the speed of, technology, most obviously the internet, and the globalisation of communications may have facilitated the spreading of the apology. Marrus refers to the effect of emulation, by which he means that a group hears of an apology in a case analogous to its own which fuels its own demand, and Weyeneth and Lazare both argue that the shrinking world of communication, 'the global village' has contributed to the globalisation of apology.[52] In relation to a case study of Japanese apologies, Yamazaki has argued that Japan has been influenced by the actions of other countries and that an apology is easier to make if others are making it; she cites the examples of German Chancellor Weizsacker's apology in 1985 concerning the Second World War and the USA government's apology in 1988 to interned Japanese-Americans as having a significant influence in Japan.[53]

While the incidence of apologies by individuals for various indiscretions and offences may not be replicated at the level of political apologies, it may be noted that technologies do seem to create new opportunities for apology. It would be a big task to chart all the reported apologies by members of the public, politicians, comedians, sportspersons, businesspeople and 'celebrities' for injudicious comments made on Facebook, Twitter and other forms of social media. It is banal yet true to note that if everyone is 'saying' more to everyone else, then the incidence of communications which may offend, and call forth an apology, will also increase.

Having examined the reasons for the rise of the apology, the next chapter will examine some of the principal issues that arise in the philosophical and political discussions around their use.

Notes

1 J. Fette, 'Apologizing for Vichy in Contemporary France', 135–63 in M. Berg and B. Schaefer (eds), *Historical Justice in International Perspective: How Societies are Trying to Right the Wrongs of the Past* (Cambridge: Cambridge University Press, 2009), pp. 135–6.

2 There is a vast literature on these themes. A sample includes M. Andrews, C. Jewitt and N. Hunt (eds), *Lest We Forget: How we Remember the Dead* (Stroud: History Press, 2011); T. G. Ashplant, G. Dawson and M. Roper (eds), *The Politics of War Memory and Commemoration* (London: Routledge, 2000); G. Cubitt, *History and Memory* (Manchester: Manchester University Press, 2007); B. Hamber, *Transforming Societies after Political Violence: Truth, Reconciliation and Mental Health* (London: Springer Dordrecht Heidelberg, 2009); P. Hazan, *Judging War, Judging History: Behind Truth and Reconciliation* (Stanford, CA: Stanford University Press, 2010); J.-W. Müller (ed.), *Memory and Power in Post-War Europe* (Cambridge: Cambridge University Press, 2002); J. K. Olick (ed.), *States of Memory: Continuities, Conflicts and Transformations in National Retrospection* (Durham, NC: Duke University Press, 2003); S. Radstone and B. Schwarz (eds), *Memory: Histories, Theories, Debates* (New York: Fordham University Press, 2010); and J. Torpey, *Making Whole What Has Been Smashed: On Reparation Politics* (Cambridge, MA: Harvard University Press, 2006).

3 See the following articles in the *Journal of Contemporary History:* C. Moriarty, 'Review article: The material culture of Great War remembrance', 34:4 (1999), 653–62; T. Cole, 'Review article: Scales of memory, layers of memory: recent work on memories of the Second World War and the Holocaust', 37:1 (2002), 129–38; J. Bourke, 'Introduction: "Remembering" war' (special issue on collective memory), 39:4 (2004), 473–85; S. Goebel, 'Review article: Beyond discourse? Bodies and memories of two World Wars', 42:2 (2007), 377–85; C. Dejung, 'Review article: A past that refuses to pass: the commemoration of the Second World War and the Holocaust', 43:4 (2008), 701–10; and G. Eley, 'The past under erasure? History, memory and the contemporary', 46:3 (2011), 555–73. One of the three sections in the 2011 edition on 'Contemporary History and the historical discipline' was entitled 'Memory, politics and publics'.

4 Torpey, *Making Whole What Has Been Smashed*, Fig. 1, p. 50.

5 *Ibid.*, p. 21.

6 See R. Teitel, *Transitional Justice* (Oxford: Oxford University Press, 2000) and N. Aiken, *Identity, Reconciliation and Transitional Justice: Overcoming Intractability in Divided Societies* (Abingdon: Routledge, 2013). For a consideration of the use of the concept, see C. Bell, C. Campbell and F. Ní Aolain, 'Transitional Justice: (re)conceptualising the field', *International Journal of Law in Context*, 3:2 (2007), 81–8.

7 See K. A. Mingst and M. P. Karns, *The United Nations in the 21st Century* (Boulder, CO: Westview Press, 3rd edn, 2007), Chapter 6.

8 Govier and Verwoerd, 'Taking wrongs seriously', p. 161.

9 Gibney and Roxstrom, 'The status of state apologies', p. 912.

10 R. B. Bilder, 'The Role of Apology in International Law', 13–30 in Gibney *et al.* (eds), *The Age of Apology*.

11 J. Torpey, 'Making whole what has been smashed: reflections on reparations', *Journal of Modern History*, 73:2 (2001), 333–58.

12 *Ibid.*, pp. 338–42.

13 Torpey, *Making Whole What Has Been Smashed*, p. 37. For another discussion of the universalisation of the Holocaust, see J. C. Alexander, 'On the Social Construction of Moral Universals: The "Holocaust" from War Crime to Trauma Drama', 196–263 in J. C. Alexander, R. Eyerman, B. Giesen, N. J. Smelser and P. Sztompka, *Cultural Trauma and Collective Identity* (Berkeley, CA, University of California Press, 2004).

14 See Nobles, *The Politics of Official Apologies*. See also Chapter 5.

15 Torpey, 'Making whole what has been smashed', p. 352.

16 Celermajer, *The Sins of the Nation*. Responsibility is discussed further in Chapter 3 and ideological positions regarding the apology in Chapter 4.

17 J. K. Olick, *The Politics of Regret: On Collective Memory and Historical Responsibility* (Abingdon: Routledge, 2007).

18 Barkan, *The Guilt of Nations*, p. 309.

19 W. Kymlicka, *Liberalism, Community and Culture* (Oxford: Oxford University Press, 1989); *Multicultural Citizenship: A Liberal Theory of Minority Rights* (Oxford: Clarendon Press, 1995).

20 J. Torpey, 'An Avalanche of History: the "Collapse of the Future" and the Rise of Reparation Politics', 21–38 in Berg and Schaefer (eds), *Historical Justice in International Perspective*, pp. 23–5.

21 F. Furedi, *Therapy Culture: Cultivating Vulnerability in an Uncertain Age* (London: Routledge, 2004), p. 19; I. Hislop, *Ian Hislop's Stiff Upper Lip – an Emotional History of Britain* (BBC 2: 2/9/16 October 2012).

22 S. Cohen, *States of Denial: Knowing about Atrocities and Suffering* (Cambridge: Polity Press, 2001), p. 292.

23 J. B. Elshtain, 'Politics and Forgiveness', 45–64 in N. Biggar (ed.), *Burying the Past: Making Peace and Doing Justice after Civil Conflict* (Washington, DC: Georgetown University Press, 2003). Lazare is also disparaging about these programmes (Lazare, *On Apology*, p. 9).

24 Torpey, 'An Avalanche of History', p. 24.

25 This term was referenced by Jonathan Freedland in 'A moment of madness?', *Guardian* (13 August 2007), www. guardian.co.uk/uk/2007/aug/13britishidentity.monarchy, accessed 9 October 2012.

26 Furedi, *Therapy Culture*, p. 18.

27 B. O' Neill, 'Misery lit … read on', http://news.bbc.co.uk/1/hi/magazine/6563529.stm, pp. 1–2, accessed 9 January 2013.

28 *Ibid.*, pp. 2–4.

29 E. West, 'Mis lit: is this the end for the misery memoir?', www.telegraph.co.uk/features/3635834/Mis-lit-Is-this-the-end-for-the-misery-memoir.html, accessed 9 January 2013; D. Aitkenhead, 'I was never about boo hoo hoo', www.guardian.co.uk/books/2008/jun/26/healthmindandbody.lifeandhealth, accessed 9 January 2013; Z. Brennan, 'A miserable liar? Angela's Ashes inspired a new literary genre – but was Frank McCourt REALLY telling the truth?', www.dailymail.co.uk/debate/article-1201062/A-miserable-liar-Angelas-Ashes-i, accessed 9 January 2013.

30 See Furedi, *Therapy Culture* for a critical account of these developments.

31 Celermajer, *The Sins of the Nation*, p. 15.

32 P. B. Hayner, *Unspeakable Truths: Facing the Challenge of Truth Commissions* (London: Routledge, 2001); P. B. Hayner, *Unspeakable Truths: Transitional Justice and the Challenge of Truth Commissions* (London: Routledge, 2nd edn, 2011). Note the addition of 'transitional justice' to the subtitle of the second edition.

33 Hayner, *Unspeakable Truths*, 2nd edn, Appendix 2, Chart 6.

34 Although these were unalike in that the German case looked at the practices of the former regime while the Yugoslavia case examined the ethnic violence in the region after the collapse of the Yugoslav state.

35 See Nobles, *The Politics of Official Apologies* for details of these countries. Aspects of the Australian and USA cases are considered in *States of Apology*, Chapter 5.

36 For more on resource mobilisation, see N. Crossley, *Making Sense of Social Movements* (Buckingham: Open University Press, 2002), Chapter 5. Nobles, *The Politics of Official Apologies* emphasises the role of political elites in the apology being realised.

37 The connection between ideology and apology is discussed further in Chapter 4.

38 Lind describes it as a 'milestone apology' because of the strength of the terms used. J. Lind, *Sorry States: Apologies in International Politics* (Ithaca, NY: Cornell University Press, 2008), p. 62. The bibliographical note provides further references to these cases.

39 'New Labour' refers to the reforms and policies associated with Blair and his supporters in attempting to make the Labour Party electable.

40 Regarding Bush, see Weisberg cited in Marrus, 'Official apologies and the quest for historical justice', p. 5.

41 Barkan, *The Guilt of Nations*, p. xvi.

42 J. Ganesh, 'Politics should not be subject to the tyranny of the apology', *Financial Times* (22 September 2012), p. 9.

43 Cited in M. Cunningham, '"It wasn't us and we didn't benefit": the discourse of opposition to an apology by Britain for its role in the slave trade', *Political Quarterly*, 79:2 (2008), 252–9, p. 255.

44 N. Watt, 'Cameron to pay respects to victims of Amritsar massacre', *Guardian* (20 February 2013), p. 6.

45 *The Times* argued that Cameron should have issued an apology. Editorial: 'An appropriate apology', *The Times* (21 February 2013), p. 2.

46 G. Parker and A. Kazmin, 'Wreath for Amritsar carries message home to voters', *Financial Times* (20 February 2013), p. 2.

47 For example, see the article by Andy Burnham, the Labour MP who had campaigned for an independent inquiry. A. Burnham, 'Handshakes, embraces, tears … the week the healing started over Hillsborough', *Observer* (16 September 2012), p. 29. Aspects of the 'Bloody Sunday' apology are also considered in Chapter 5.

48 Watt, 'Cameron to pay respects to victims of Amritsar massacre'.

49 Figures given by Cameron in House of Commons statement (Hansard, 6th Series, vol. 511, cols 734–61, 15 June 2010).

50 Angus Reid, 'Britons and Northern Irish welcome PMs apology for Bloody Sunday', www.angus-reid.com/polls…/britons-and-northern-irish-welcome-p, accessed 29 November 2012.

51 At the time of the apology, some Unionist representatives wanted a parallel recognition and acknowledgement of other deaths resulting from the Troubles. See also Chapter 5.

52 Marrus, 'Official apologies and the quest for historical justice', p. 22; Weyeneth, 'The power of apology and the process of historical reconciliation', pp. 36–7; Lazare, *On Apology*, pp. 11–14. Weyeneth also argues that the approach of the millennium may have influenced religious organisations and their apologies; presumably this would be a less significant factor in state apologies.

53 J. W. Yamazaki, *Japanese Apologies for World War II: A Rhetorical Study* (Abingdon: Routledge, 2006), p. 113.

3

The apology: the principal issues

As indicated in the introduction, a reading of academic material on the political apology and a review of journalistic and popular responses to particular cases of apology suggest that academics writing about the topic tend to be supportive of the idea of the apology. By supportive I mean that they believe that the political apology can be defended as a coherent idea and that it has the potential to produce good political outcomes, such as the promotion of justice or reconciliation. By contrast, the 'popular' response to the apology is often more sceptical, if not cynical, doubting both its coherence and practical value.[1] This is, of course, a generalisation and the degree of scepticism varies with different apologies.

For those who wish to make a defence of the apology there are four issues that need to be addressed because they occur in many, if not all, cases of political apology and are often the basis for a sceptical or critical assault on the apology. These are the issues of responsibility, time, indeterminacy and sincerity. These issues are particularly pertinent, I would argue, because they often feature both in popular critiques and have also been the focus of academic consideration and, therefore, act as a bridge or link between the two spheres. The following sections will review these issues in turn.

'We didn't do it': the question of responsibility

In many cases of political apology the politician or statesperson making the apology was not in office when the injustice for which the apology is being made took place and in many cases he or she was not alive. Similarly, many or all of the current citizens of the state were not alive. Therefore, the issue of responsibility becomes immediately apparent and means that the defenders of the principle of the apology have to deal with the question of how one can apologise for something for which one was not responsible, and possibly preceded one's existence. It was argued in Chapter 1 that responsibility is a key part of the apology so this is a central concern.

The political apology, in a sense, forces us to think about collective responsibility and intergenerational responsibility. As a starting point it is worth thinking about aspects of responsibility at the level of the interpersonal apology for comparison. Generally, we do not apologise if we were not responsible. In 'everyday' English, it makes sense to say that you are sorry to hear that a friend's mother is ill but it would be meaningless to apologise for this situation since that would imply responsibility. As Gill and Miller, amongst others, have pointed out our personal apologies do sometimes extend beyond our direct responsibility in that people apologise for the unruly behaviour of their children or their pets which foul a neighbour's lawn.[2] Presumably, the reason people do this is that their perception of their relationship to their children and their pets means they are prepared to take responsibility. (However, it may be objected that, unlike the political connections to be considered below, these apologies are made on behalf of those who cannot understand the concept of responsibility.)

Despite these codicils, it seems that in Anglo-American culture the liberal idea of the autonomous individual is strongly embedded which means that the idea of apologising for that for which one is not responsible is incoherent and morally dubious. So supporters of the political apology have to think about how the idea of a collective apology might work.[3] One way to examine these ideas is to consider how it is argued that the state can apologise and/or that people as members of political communities (citizens) or as members of national communities can apologise, and some of the problems with these formulations. Empirically, apologies by states, citizens and members of national communities can overlap and be intertwined; however, analytically it is useful to consider them separately.

First, let us consider how it may be meaningful for the state to apologise. As indicated above, liberal conceptions of responsibility may sit uneasily with extensive collective responsibility. Various factors may impact upon how far the idea of collective responsibility extends; for example how organised the collective is, whether it has formal membership, whether it has a legal status and the ethos or culture informing its operations. Many philosophers would find it reasonable for the president or CEO of a company to be held responsible (e.g. to be subject to legal action or obliged to apologise) for an illegal or immoral act carried out by company members or employees before his or her term of office. This can be defended on the basis of the clear institutional continuity of the company structure over time. Similarly, it would not seem unreasonable to hold an army officer responsible for illegal torture carried out by a junior member of his or her unit (without the officer's knowledge or permission), given the formal and hierarchical nature of military organisations. The issue of collective responsibility would seem to become more complex when the collective or organisation involved is more informal or diffuse; for example, how far can anyone who participates in the activities of a mob, perhaps on the fringes, be held responsible for the most violent actions associated with it?[4]

If the presence of clear institutional and organisational continuity is an important underpinning for the taking of responsibility by agents who were not directly responsible for a particular injustice, this can support the idea of the state apology, at least in certain circumstances. This can be illustrated by two examples which have been cited in Chapter 2. In 2010 Prime Minister David Cameron apologised for 'Bloody Sunday' which happened in 1972 when he was not in office and was, in fact, still a child. The reason he could do this was because as the current Prime Minister his office allowed, or obliged, him to apologise for the actions of the British state from an earlier period. In 1997, Tony Blair apologised for the British state's failings in relation to the Irish Potato Famine of the 1840s. There are significant differences in the two apologies, however they are directly comparable in respect of state continuity. The British state at the time of the apologies had a clear and unambiguous continuity with the British state of the 1840s and of the 1970s.

It can be argued that state continuity is one possible way to ground the argument for a state apology. However, it also seems to have two limitations which is why most writers on apology have tried to reformulate and extend the idea of transgenerational responsibility.

First, few contemporary states have an unambiguous or uncontested continuity with past states. Leaving aside exactly how we define state continuity, the upheavals of the First and Second World Wars and the collapse of the Soviet Union mean that very few contemporary European states can be viewed fundamentally as continuous with those in existence, for example, in 1914. New constitutions, independence from multi-national empires and transitions from fascist or authoritarian rule to democracy have radically transformed most of them. Independence for colonies after the Second World War and transitions from authoritarian states mean that in many extra-European parts of the world there have also been massive ruptures and discontinuities.

The significance of this is that if the apology were rooted solely in the institutional continuity of states, many potential apologies could or would not be addressed. On this basis, Germany or the former West Germany or East Germany, could plausibly claim to have nothing or little to do with Nazi Germany and, as the current French Republic was founded in 1958, its representatives could claim that the Vichy state had nothing to do with contemporary France. Similarly, democratic and non-militarised contemporary Japan could distance itself from its imperial past, despite the continuation of the Emperor as Head of State. It is worth noting here that these three countries do not adopt this position which suggests that institutional political continuity is not empirically important to the way in which states conceive of their past.

The second limitation of thinking about the apology in relation to state continuity, and in particular institutional continuity, is that it does not consider the role of the demos, the people, whether this role is explored as people being members of a political community (citizens) or as members of a national community. Hypothetically, a state might apologise for an injustice because it accepts that state continuity implies a duty to apologise even if none of its citizens accepts the idea of transgenerational responsibility and thus holds that the injustice has nothing to do with them. In practice, this is unlikely if not impossible. In Chapter 2, it was recorded that only democracies tend to apologise. It thus seems implausible that a democratic state would apologise if the wider political culture and opinion of the demos rejected the concept of responsibility. There would be no public support for such an apology and the disjuncture between the people and the state would potentially challenge the representative legitimacy of that state. Even if the apology could take place under such conditions, the impact of it on the recipients would most likely be reduced or vitiated because it would be clear that the citizens of the state in no way endorsed it.

If we move to the 'level' of the people, that is, beyond the responsibility of the state as institution, it is clear that most writers about the apology believe that the idea of transgenerational responsibility is valid. This is because any current citizen is a member of a political community that exists over time; citizenship and political community are not constituted afresh with each generation.

It is useful to consider some of the implications and limitations to this way of thinking. As a normative question, it may be phrased 'Why should I as a British citizen (or subject) feel responsible for what happened in the past?'

One answer may be constructed around the benefits, material or otherwise, that have accrued from membership. An example is that of British imperialism. Although the impact of imperialism is a highly contested topic, it can be argued that imperialism was both politically unjustifiable and a system of political relations that greatly benefited Britain's economic development, particularly in the nineteenth century. If Britain is a richer country today because of imperialism, as a citizen I cannot reasonably argue that imperialism has nothing to do with me. If, additionally, it can be demonstrated that British imperialism adversely impacted on the economic development of a colonised country it would be reasonable for me, as a current British citizen, to endorse an apology and forms of material reparation to that country.

Another example of how current membership has the corollary of collective responsibility is developed by Celermajer.[5] The public culture of Australia has for long periods endorsed, or failed actively to oppose, the practices and structures that maintained indigenous Australians' disadvantage. The responsibility for this state of affairs was a collective one as it was institutionally and culturally embedded and current citizens have colluded in such practices.

It is likely, though hard to quantify, that some past injustices will have benefited some current citizens more than others, in material or other ways. It is also possible that particular injustices may not have benefited past or current members of the political community. However, this is not, in principle, important to most conceptions of collective responsibility based on citizenship. It is as citizens *qua* citizens that we have a responsibility for addressing wrongs and apologising for what went before. It should also be noted that the majority of supporters of collective responsibility do not believe that emotions such as guilt, remorse or shame are necessarily related to the concept. Examples include Thompson and Weiner who endorse Arendt's distinction that collective political responsibility is a coherent concept whereas collective guilt is not.[6]

It is possible to argue for political responsibility based on a 'thin' concept of citizenship. By this is meant that the citizen has certain rights and responsibilities as a member of a state (e.g. the holding of a passport, the obligation to do military service and to pay taxes, and the right to claim forms of welfare). In relation to the apology, the current citizen can and should apologise because he or she is a member of a polity which has committed an injustice; his or her current status as a citizen forms the link to the past. This is why, for example, Weiner criticises the academic and journalist Camille Paglia's claim that slavery in the USA has nothing to do with her (she was not responsible) and neither were her ancestors responsible since all her grandparents were born in Italy and had nothing to do with the practices of nineteenth-century USA. It is her status as an American citizen that is the important factor here.[7] Thompson makes a similar point in arguing that newly arrived immigrants or descendants of those who were guiltless are unlikely to feel shame or guilt; however they share responsibility in relation to apology or reparation because of their status as a citizen.[8] Miller makes the point that if one is not a citizen of a particular country, and resides, for example, as a refugee it would be reasonable to exempt such a person from bearing the cost of rectification for an injustice or partaking in an apology.

This concept of political citizenship says nothing about the cultural or national aspects or attributes of citizenship. An argument for political responsibility can be built upon this; however it is useful to expand the analysis to take account of the empirical reality that many states have a national identity and a set of cultural practices which impact upon the idea of what it is to be a citizen and imbue the identities of citizens.[9] There may, of course, be much debate about what constitutes the national and public culture of a particular state or whether it can, or should, take multiple forms, particularly in states with diverse ethnic and linguistic groupings. The significance here is that the wider cultural identity of the citizen, including the holding of a national identity, can be utilised to construct a defence of transgenerational and collective responsibility.

The employment of national identity as the basis for an argument that responsibility crosses generations uses, implicitly or explicitly, the communitarian critique of the liberal conceptualisation of the self. This is a large and complex area so what follows is a brief summary.[10] The communitarian 'school' may not always speak with one voice, however some common ideas may be identified. Communitarian thinkers argue that the liberal conceptualisation of the self is inadequate in that it abstracts and universalises ideas about human motivation and self-understanding (and also how people should think about justice and fairness) in a way that is ontologically and empirically unconvincing. For communitarians, we are, as individuals, necessarily constituted by a complex of social, cultural and historical linkages – this is what we are. We cannot 'step outside' or 'back from' these connections to discover some unencumbered and autonomous self as posited by liberal theory.

To put it crudely, liberal conceptions of the self emphasise more the scope of choice to decide 'who we are' and what our commitments and obligations are, or should be, than does the communitarian tradition. It is probably already clear how such a conceptualisation of the self and one's commitments and obligations can be employed in a defence of transgenerational responsibility and the apology.

In an article written in 1999, I quoted Alasdair MacIntyre as a thinker who encapsulated these ideas about the self and commitments. He stated: 'I inherit from the past of my family, my city, my nation, a variety of debts, inheritances, rightful expectations and obligations … the story of my life is always embedded in the story of those communities from which I derive an identity. I am born with a past; and to try to cut myself off from that past … is to deform my present relationships.'[11]

That MacIntyre's formulation is useful for those wishing to advocate the idea of collective and transgenerational responsibility is borne out in that the same or adjacent text is cited in three recent works which are sympathetic to the idea. Of these works one is specifically about apology and the other two consider apology in the course of a wider discussion of responsibility and obligation.[12]

Let us expand a little on how these communitarian ideas can be used in service of the apology. There are two aspects in particular that can be utilised. First, if we accept MacIntyre's idea of self and of obligation it is impossible to claim that the past has nothing to with us. Second, as virtually all people are members of nation-states (or nations which would like to become nation-states) it is difficult, if not impossible to claim that the past of our nation has nothing to do with us. (The fact that one may have many other loyalties, commitments and obligations to other non-national groupings or associations or be critical of aspects of nationalism or national identification does not invalidate this point.)

Here, then, is the move from responsibility based upon political citizenship to one based on national membership. Miller argues that this formulation has two advantages; many injustices were undertaken by peoples and national communities, not by states, and national continuity is often more long-lasting and easier to identify than the political continuity of states, as already indicated.[13]

The literature that supports the idea of transgenerational responsibility as underpinning the apology often contains both a normative and empirical dimension. We (members of a national community) should take responsibility for past injustices committed by the community and, in practice, we do feel attachments to previous generations of our national community. As Sandel claims, forms of moral and political obligation are commonly recognised among people including that of historic memory.[14]

One assumes that the extent to which a national community identifies, and in what way, with its past is varied and may depend on many political and cultural variables. However, one can find examples that make these claims plausible. Some French people clearly identify with the republican principles of France established in the late eighteenth century, some take pride in the contribution of France to the world of cuisine and some take pride in the exploits of the resistance to Nazi occupation. These examples predate the existence of the current French Republic, the current political entity, so the identification is based on a narrative continuity of French identity. Similarly, some Germans are proud of the contribution to world literature of Schiller and Goethe and to philosophy of Kant and Hegel, to whom they are connected as Germans and not by membership of the same or continuous political entity.

However, to be consistent one cannot choose only the 'good bits'. Pride in, or identification with, the examples above means, or should mean, recognition of connection to the unjust past actions of the nation.[15] If one celebrates Republican principles and the Resistance one must also confront the legacy of the Vichy Regime and the colonial brutalities of Algeria. If one celebrates German cultural contributions one must also confront the legacy of the Holocaust. As one commentator has noted, John Howard could not reasonably celebrate and identify with Don Bradman's batting prowess and maintain that discrimination against indigenous people had nothing to do with him (Howard) as an Australian.[16]

Two concluding thoughts will be offered. First, there will be cases of past injustice which cannot be rectified, or apologies given, even if the principle of national responsibility outlined here were widely accepted and employed. There may be no surviving people or national members of a group who share that link with the perpetrators of the original injustice. It may also be the case that in certain countries the strength of localised or regional identities undermines or qualifies the forging of a national, narrative identity. We may meaningfully talk of a Spanish national identity, yet would contemporary Galicians feel responsible for a past hypothetical injustice carried out principally by Andalucians, or members of the Basque country for one carried out by Castilians?

Second, it is possible to make an analogy with the personal apology. As indicated earlier in this chapter, we do sometimes apologise for our children, other family members or pets because we have a form of identification with, and attachment to, them that makes us accept this responsibility. If we have a political identification with, and attachment to, previous generations of the nation we can, likewise, accept the responsibility and make it manifest through the political apology. There is a significant difference in that children and pets do not understand the concept of responsibility while previous generations did; that said, this identification with previous generations may allow us to apologise on their behalf.

'It was all so long ago': the question of time

The principal issue to be addressed here is whether or how the passage of time affects the claim for an apology. Clearly, there is no simple definition of time or what constitutes a 'long time'. Time is socially and culturally constructed and understood differently in pre-modern or pre-industrial epochs than in contemporary societies and much of the literature about the contested concept 'globalisation' emphasises the compression of time in an age of instant communication. It is also the case that as well as differing between cultures and societies, concepts and understandings of time may differ within the same society because of its conceptualisation in different spheres of activity.

It is useful, for comparison, to think about time in other spheres and see if some of the intuitions or arguments help to illuminate a discussion of the apology. As in other chapters, a comparison with the personal apology will be offered. The phrase 'time is a healer' or 'time is a great healer' suggests that there is a popular view that time makes a difference and that the passage of time lessens the impact of particular wrongs or hurts. To return to a previous example, it would seem strange if I were to apologise to my partner for missing dinner through staying too long in the pub thirty years after the event. It is unlikely that she would remember the particular incident and if it had been of great importance it would have surfaced years earlier. However, the seriousness of the transgression may be an important factor in the consideration. If thirty years ago I had defrauded or physically harmed my brother it is highly unlikely that he would have forgotten the incident and an apology, even after such a long period, could be considered a reasonable and proper response.

Similar understandings often inform the judicial sphere. The concept of a 'statute of limitations' in British law applies to civil cases and not to criminal offences. There may be pragmatic reasons relating to problems about the reliability of evidence for not pursuing long-past crimes but this is not based on a jurisprudential principle. In Britain, police forces often re-open investigations to long-past crimes on the basis of their perceived seriousness, suggesting that the seriousness of a transgression (a personal one relating to apology or a criminal act) is a factor on how long it remains pertinent and worthy of correction or calling to account. The American legal system does not recognise a statute of limitations for serious crimes, or what in the USA are known as heinous crimes. Similarly, international law does not recognise a statute of limitations for war crimes, crimes against humanity or genocide. As with our sense of personal transgressions, jurisprudence and judicial practice recognise that the seriousness of the wrong or transgression can be an important factor.

Another area worthy of consideration is that of compensation and reparation. This is because these are areas that relate both to the judicial sphere and are, or can be, closely linked to the issue of apology and, in one sense, provide a bridge between them. The debates within this area are long and complex; a summary will be given here of some of the questions that are raised.[17]

The majority of philosophers considering this issue argue that the passage of time does make a difference to claims for compensation or reparation and weakens the case for them. Let us consider the following example. If my father has material assets or holdings stolen from him or if I have material assets or holdings stolen from me, most philosophers and writers on jurisprudence argue that I have a claim to compensation. This is, in part, because my assets or holdings, or those of my father which I had reason to believe would be bequeathed to me, provide the basis for me to pursue a particular form of life and the expectations therein. If they are unjustly taken from me (through, for example, theft, fraud or extortion) I have a claim, moral and legal, for compensation. It follows from this that if a direct ancestor of mine was defrauded twenty generations ago my claim is reduced or invalid on these grounds because I cannot reasonably think about my expectations, or my entitlements, in relation to what my position would be now if an illegal transaction had not taken place so long ago. Relatedly, over a period of centuries that would have transpired in this example, there have been so many transactions and counter-factuals, it is implausible that I have a strong claim on compensation. It should be noted that with the passage of time it is more difficult to provide proof of the wrong, the fraud or theft that would satisfy a court of law. However, this is not the issue here since, even if the evidence was not in dispute, it is my distance from the original wrong in itself that weakens my claim to compensation.

One could accept the argument that an individual's claim for material compensation is rendered weaker or invalid by the passage of time. However this would not necessarily be a convincing argument in relation to apology and the experience of collectives. This can be illustrated by the example of the treatment of indigenous peoples.

An argument can be made that an apology to the indigenous people of Australia by the Australian government and by the USA government to Native Americans is intellectually coherent and morally just because the original injustices (which some might consider to be 'a long time ago') of land seizures and dispossession, and associated brutalities, have a contemporary resonance. These are both material in that contemporary members of the group have suffered economically because of the legacy of institutional and structural discrimination and psychological because of the membership of and identification with a marginalised group. This type of analysis would allow one to argue that time 'dissolves' in that there is a much stronger link between past injustice and contemporary experience than the example of my claim as an individual above recognises. This position is argued by Thompson who states: 'a history that connects earlier and later injustices is not merely a chronicle of events. It is a narrative that makes sense of events at a particular time by reference to later or earlier happenings. What counts as harm, what kind of harm it is, depends on the way in which people understand their history.'[18]

A related point is that if the issue is considered in relation to the collective, in this case indigenous peoples, it can be argued that it is not necessary, and is anyway impossible, to evaluate the position of each current member had things been different. If it can be plausibly argued that either the original dispossession of lands or the subsequent treatment of these communities, or both actions or series of actions, constituted an injustice then an apology is justified. It can also be argued that some form of collective compensation would be appropriate to recognise, and to underpin the sincerity of, the apology.

The general argument for a statute of limitations to the apology is not convincing. As Brooks has argued, the concept is a legalistic one which does not transfer readily to the moral sphere of the apology.[19] There are two other drawbacks to its application. One is that there is no way of deciding what would be the 'cut off' point for apologies in principle and the second is that if the idea of a statute of limitations gained purchase it could be invoked by groups in attempts to avoid being called to account for injustices because they happened 'a long time ago'.

It should be emphasised here that there may be long-distant events that do not require apologies or that long-distant events may be considered injustices but no apology will be forthcoming, and cannot occur, because no current group or institution is responsible (see section above on responsibility). The point here is that time, the length of time ago, is not *of itself* the reason to disqualify the apology. This can be illustrated by some examples.

In a 1999 article I claimed that reparation for the Norman conquest of Britain in the eleventh century would seem ludicrous and Joyce, in the same year, cited the same example and argued there was no need for an apology because the English have 'got over it'. He pithily noted that 'the question of whether an apology *should* take place depends partly on whether anyone *cares*'.[20] This is also nicely illustrated by an example cited by Thaler in which the response of the Irish to an apology from the Danish government for Viking raids was one of bemusement and appreciative comments about the quality of a replica ship that sailed to Dublin in commemoration.[21] Although time is a factor in these cases, it does not seem to me to be the determining one. Joyce's point is a pertinent one; if no individual or group considers an injustice to have happened, or that one happened but it has no contemporary legacy or resonance, then an apology is unnecessary. Another example will illustrate the point. Hypothetically, in 500 years time an Armenian community or people may still exist which demands an apology from the Turkish state for the Armenian genocide of the early twentieth century. This would be unlike the Norman conquest example in that one can identify a group wanting an apology and, on the grounds of responsibility developed above, a group which should provide it. Therefore, despite the long passage of time, the call for an apology is meaningful, which serves to reinforce the argument that time *per se* is not the issue in these cases.

'Apologise to whom?': the question of indeterminacy

Having considered the question of responsibility above which partly entails the question 'Who should or can apologise?' this section considers the 'other side of the coin', in that the question of to whom should an apology be made is considered. A related question is whether it matters if the victims of an injustice cannot be easily defined or identified.

Let us start with the proposition that has been implicit or explicit in most of the discussion. Those who are victims of an injustice have a legitimate claim for an apology. This immediately raises the question of how can a victim be identified. Particular examples will serve to illustrate the possible problems and complexities of such identification.

The first example is the Hillsborough disaster of 1989 which was mentioned in Chapter 2. It was a specific and recent incident which suggests *prima facie* that the victims of the injustice should be easy to recognise. However, some reflection challenges this assumption. That those killed and injured at Hillsborough were victims seems beyond dispute or challenge. Two other groups which suffered can be identified; those who witnessed the events and consequently suffered psychological ill-health or trauma of various kinds and the relatives of those who died or were injured. A fourth group for consideration is Liverpool supporters who mourned the loss of ninety-six of their fellow supporters. It would be insensitive to compare their suffering or their being classified as potential victims in the manner of the families; however it is not self-evidently wrong to include them. By analogy, people can feel grief and loss when co-nationals die in wars or other events and people with strong religious identities can feel grief and loss in relation to the death of co-religionists. These feelings are based on a sense of identity or connection that does not depend on personal connections or relationships; in Anderson's oft-cited phrase nations are 'imagined communities'.[22] Given the strength of some people's allegiance to a football club, it is by no means clear that if the example of national or religious identification has any merit, it cannot be extended to the 'imagined community' of football. The picture may be more nuanced than this in that natives of Liverpool may have felt a loss connected to the death of fellow Liverpudlians even if not part of that football club's 'imagined community'. Various representatives of Liverpool FC and the families involved went on record in relation to support given by Everton FC, the other major football team in Liverpool and Liverpool's rivals, and Evertonians.

This example suggests that the identification of victims of an injustice is not straightforward and beyond contention even for recent events. When the injustice affected collectives rather than individuals and happened longer ago the identification of victims becomes yet more difficult. Two examples illustrate this point; those of the Irish Famine and slavery in the USA.

Who were, or are, the victims of the Irish Famine? Those who died or survived in a malnourished state and suffered long-term physical impairment would be included. The issue of emigration is more problematic. Those forced to move thousands of miles from their homeland could be considered victims; however how would their subsequent experiences or 'life chances' be evaluated in relation to the issue? For example, an Irish emigrant to the USA who emigrates unwillingly and then achieves material success or status unlikely to have occurred given his or her economic or social position in Ireland. It seems difficult, if not impossible, to weigh the physical and possible psychological hardship of emigration against the material or other rewards which were a direct result of the emigrant's move to a new country. What of the second- or third-generation Irish-American whose sense of Irish identity remains so strong that it is a source of constant stress or psychological disturbance that he or she cannot live in Ireland; again, how could one meaningfully evaluate this?

It is argued by some that the Irish Famine was an event of such a scale and of such significance that it is a collective, national form of trauma and thus the victims include, or potentially include, Irish people of successive generations.[23] However, if one examines the impact of the Famine at the level of individual advantage, it is unlikely, empirically, that all Irish people were victims given that the subsequent depopulation allowed the consolidation of farmland and holdings to the benefit of certain individuals or agrarian classes. Hypothetically, an individual in mid to late nineteenth-century Ireland might have benefited materially from the socio-economic changes wrought by the Famine, in which he or she took pleasure and comfort, and simultaneously have felt hurt and pain at witnessing the distress of his or her compatriots.

The issue of slavery within the USA contains some of the same elements as in the Irish example; one significant difference being the degree of contemporary resonance including the variety of political positions and the strength of political feeling that the issue generates. Those enslaved were clearly victims of injustice; the issue of much debate and interpretation is how far the injustice stretches.[24] Contemporary African-Americans can be viewed as victims of slavery, or as recipients of injustice if the term 'victim' has overly passive overtones, in two ways. First, the contemporary socio-economic position of the African-American community in general is related to the legacy of slavery. Second, that contemporary African-Americans suffer in non-material ways, including forms of collective trauma, through racism which is linked to the legacy of slavery. It hardly needs emphasising that these two positions or claims are contentious and the subject of much dispute; a dispute in which both entrenched political positions and reasoned and reasonable empirical claims stand in opposition. For example, even if one accepted that the contemporary socio-economic position were linked to past disadvantage and discrimination, this might entail a much more complex consideration of the relationship between slavery and other later practices and institutions such as segregation and Jim Crow laws.[25]

At a more fundamental level is the question of the constitution of the group or the collective. 'Race' is not fixed biologically but is socially constructed and subject to reconstruction and re-interpretation as it is used, for example, to challenge existing hierarchies or for political mobilisation. Therefore, the category of African-American is not fixed.

More could be said to illustrate this point, including the interesting though rather arcane point that without the institution of slavery most African-Americans would not have existed so their former or current position must be measured against the counter-factual of non-existence. However, it has been demonstrated that the identification of to whom an apology is owed is far from straightforward.

The question of indeterminacy is related to different conceptualisations and interpretive frameworks that will be regularly encountered in any reflective consideration of the apology. In particular these include an individualistic construction of responsibility and justice which informs much liberal political thought and jurisprudence and a more collective, often identity-based, construction of justice, memory and hurt which informs much communitarian thought and influences some schools of psychology. An example of this latter way of thinking is found in Govier who argues that: 'One does not have to be personally harassed, looted or beaten to be harmed. *Distributively*, we may say in such a case that individual members of a group have been harmed because of what has happened to other individuals within it.'[26] Therefore, how one defines or conceptualises the victim of an injustice will, ultimately, depend on which of these frameworks one finds more intellectually or politically convincing.

The question remains to be addressed of whether indeterminacy undermines the apology. In one way, it could be considered a strength of the apology. If we assume no consensus can be reached on exactly who constitutes victims, an apology can be accepted (or not) by any of those who feel themselves to be a victim of an injustice. If the US President were to apologise for slavery he could not prescribe who should, and who should not, count themselves as legitimate recipients of the apology. Ultimately, whether I would wish to include myself as a member of group or a collective to whom an apology is made is up to me and a subjective issue.[27]

There are two possible problems with such an 'open-ended' apology; i.e. where there is no consensus concerning the victims. These can be deemed practical and political rather than philosophical. One is that this type of apology may weaken support for the idea of the apology among the demos on the grounds that it is ill-defined and nebulous. Second, because compensation, or compensation to individuals, is unlikely to be forthcoming with this form of apology, the recipients may find it inadequate and it may not have the reconciliatory or other desired effects that the government had intended.

A comparison between the apology to Japanese-Americans interned during the Second World War and the lack of a presidential apology for slavery in the USA will help to illustrate these points. The apology to Japanese-Americans took place because it fulfilled four criteria. First, there was a clearly identifiable group who had suffered an injustice; therefore the indeterminacy question was not salient. Second, because the group was clearly identifiable compensation could be offered to individuals within the constraints of a liberal jurisprudential concept of whom is eligible for compensation. Third, there was political support for, or no concerted and mobilised opposition to, the apology by the government of the USA and, fourth, the financial costs of compensation were not overly burdensome for the US treasury.

All four criteria are absent in the case of slavery which goes some way to explain why no presidential apology has been forthcoming. The recipients of the apology are not clearly identifiable, therefore there are no clearly identified individuals who could claim compensation, it is likely that there would be significant political opposition to the apology and some have argued that an apology might lead to law suits arguing that an apology implied government responsibility and would lead to significant financial implications for the US government.[28]

Therefore, for a mixture of ideological and political reasons it appears generally unlikely that apologies, or potential apologies, involving indeterminacy will result in compensation or reparation for individuals. This is not to say that these apologies are without merit or substance. The apology of itself or the apology combined with collective forms of reparation may be either realisable or desirable. If governments find compensation to individuals who are generationally, or in other ways, removed from the original injustice ideologically unacceptable or politically lacking in support, they can, and do, offer two other types of reparation. One form is the commemorative by which public buildings, museums, exhibitions, statues, etc. mark the public recognition of the injustice and the other is the adoption of policies which address the contemporary collective impact of an injustice, through, for example, affirmative action in areas of education and employment.[29]

'Cheap words': the question of sincerity

A frequently raised criticism of the political apology is that it is cheap and easy; that the person making it is not sincere and/or that it is a 'low cost' form of reparation or restitution. It should be noted that these objections are logically distinct but often get run together. To explore this issue, it is worth, once again, to make comparison with the personal apology.

Most commentators argue that some emotional engagement is either desirable or necessary in the construction of a personal apology. Given that the relationship between the parties is often close, and one objective is often to restore relations, an expression of remorse, regret, shame or guilt is both reasonable to expect and will be efficacious in repairing relations. A potential practical problem arises in judging whether the professed emotions are real in that it is quite possible that the apologiser is being falsely contrite and faking the emotional engagement. If we define sincerity to be the feeling of a requisite emotion, whether we believe a personal apology to be sincere may well depend on our relationship to, and assessment of, the person offering the apology. This is one reason why the personal apology is often accompanied by something material which underpins the apology. For example, the giving of flowers does not prove the sincerity (the genuineness) of the professed emotion; however the gift may help to convince the recipient of the meaningfulness of the apology in that the apologiser has both provided some material recompense (and spent some money) and has bought something that is culturally recognisable as a symbol of apology.

How do these ideas relate to the sphere of politics? It is important here to distinguish between three different kinds of apology made by politicians. First, if a politician insults a friend or is unfaithful to his or her partner then any apology would be a personal or interpersonal one and would thus categorically be considered the same as any other interpersonal apology and subject to the same criteria which governs these. Second, there is the apology made by a politician in relation to a statement made or policy enacted in his or her role as a politician. It can be argued that this form of apology is a 'halfway house' between the interpersonal apology and the political apology under discussion here. Since the apology is coming from the person directly responsible for the statement or action, it is crucially different from the apology made by a head of state for an historical injustice or even a recent one that preceded his or her tenure. However, it is also different from an interpersonal apology. In September 2012 Nick Clegg, the Liberal Democrat leader and member of the Coalition government in the UK, apologised for a commitment made before he was in government to oppose any increase in student tuition fees. This apology was made on the basis that it was not a commitment he could keep when in office and thus it should not have been made. This apology seems reasonable in that Clegg clearly had the status to make the apology as he had made the earlier claim. (The fact that many of his party and its voters were not mollified because his apology was not for the policy that they disliked but for the unsustainable commitment is not the issue here.)

It can be argued that Clegg could reasonably feel regret for a political judgement and accept blame for it; he was responsible and thus a certain emotional engagement could be deemed appropriate or necessary. However, it seems unlikely that we would expect either the degree or type of emotional engagement in this case that Clegg would, or should, display in apology for a transgression which related to his personal life rather than to his political judgement.

The third type of apology, the 'political apology' is that made by politicians, often as head of state, for injustices in which they were not directly involved, although as outlined in the first section of this chapter they can be considered to have a responsibility to address. As discussed, these can be of recent standing or from the distant past. In these cases, it has become a majority position in recent literature that emotions, and emotional engagement, are not applicable to the political apology because it is of a different type to the personal where emotions and emotional engagement, if not always present, are applicable.[30]

If the argument that the emotions are irrelevant in the giving of a political apology is correct, it follows logically that emotions cannot be used as a touchstone or indicator of the sincerity of the apology. This leaves two questions to be addressed; how might the sincerity of an apology be measured or demonstrated and why might this matter.

The sincerity of the apology can be demonstrated by the 'follow-up' or to put it more formally, in a consequentialist manner. To use Thaler's phrase, the political apology can be conceived of as 'agent independent' in that the motivations or engagement of the apologiser is not the issue but the sincerity lies in the outcomes that the apology produces.[31]

This will be illustrated through examples of different types of political apology. Let us return to the example of the Hillsborough disaster. If this way of thinking about political apologies is correct, it would not be expected, or indeed appropriate, for David Cameron to feel guilt, shame or remorse about the events. However, having taken responsibility as Prime Minister and made a formal, public apology, it is reasonable to expect that actions would accompany or follow the apology. It is not easy to give a precise list of what these might be as they might be subject to legal restraints and would appropriately be discussed and negotiated with the families of the victims. However, possible examples include a new inquest, possible legal or disciplinary action against those shown to be culpable or negligent at the time or involved in the subsequent 'cover up' and financial compensation.

In the case of intra-state apologies to a minority group which has been the victim of discrimination, various programmes and policies should be enacted to ensure that the group has the full benefits of citizenship. Apologies are context-specific so a definitive list of these is not possible but could include programmes of economic regeneration and reform, affirmative action and attempts to address elements of cultural, educational and symbolic practices that have excluded minority group recognition.[32]

The third type of apology is the inter-state one. Both Thaler and Nobles are concerned with the intra-state apology and different issues and dynamics are involved with apologies between states. The most obvious one is that in inter-state apologies there is neither the sense of responsibility to one's own citizens nor the imperative, either moral or political, to apologise as part of a strategy to recognise their standing as citizens. Also, there is a strong tradition of realism in international relations that would not recognise the role of moral or political responsibility to another state.[33]

However one could make the same proviso that in cases of inter-state apology actions should be taken that demonstrate a recasting of relations. These, again, are context-specific but examples include the relinquishing of former territorial claims, the improved treatment of national minorities within the state, revised or expanded forms of trade and economic exchange, reparation, returning of cultural artefacts and the funding of inter-state educational and cultural exchanges.

The final point to address is why might the sincerity of the apology matter. The answer is that it does not if one adheres to a strongly realist view of politics whereby statecraft as an activity and discipline sits outside moral considerations. However, most proponents of the apology, if not all of an idealist school, work with some conception of liberal-democracies being guided by principles that would oblige them to rectify past injustice, or at least attempt to, and to strive to ensure an inclusive conception of citizenship. If the apology has a part to play in this, then it is a practice to be defended.[34] Part of this defence is to argue for the coherence of the idea and to prevent it falling into disrepute as a cheap, cynical ploy by presenting some criteria by which its sincerity can be judged.

While a degree of scepticism is useful, an overly cynical view of apologies may be corrosive. At a time when the stock of British politicians is low in the wake of the expenses scandal and their foreign counterparts are not held in high esteem, it is useful to try to lay out some criteria to judge the apology so not all are derided or dismissed by a sceptical public.[35] One does not have to be overly idealistic or naive to argue that the problem with political cynicism is that it ultimately corrodes and renders futile representative politics, democratic engagement and active citizenship if much of the demos comes to believe the entire political class to be self-serving or without principle.

Notes

1 Among works detailing public scepticism are Barkan and Karn, 'Group Apology as an Ethical Imperative'; Cunningham, '"It wasn't us and we didn't benefit"'; Gibney and Roxstrom, 'The status of state apologies'; Govier and Verwoerd, 'Taking wrongs seriously'; Smith, *I Was Wrong*; Thaler, 'Just pretending'; J. Thompson, 'Apology, Justice and Respect: A Critical Defense of Political Apology', 31–44 in Gibney *et al.* (eds), *The Age of Apology*; and Weyeneth, 'The power of apology and the process of historical reconciliation'.

2 Gill, 'The moral functions of an apology', p. 13; D. Miller, *National Responsibility and Global Justice* (Oxford: Oxford University Press, 2007), p. 157. Also see Chapter 6 of Miller for a useful discussion of responsibility across generations.

3 Smith argues that most philosophers working on the apology find the idea of group responsibility and collective apologies unproblematic. See Smith, *I Was Wrong*, pp. 176–7.

4 *Ibid.* See Chapter 10 for a more detailed consideration of collective responsibility.
5 Celermajer, *The Sins of the Nation.*
6 Thompson, 'Apology, Justice and Respect', p. 36; Weiner, *Sins of the Parents*, pp. 116–18.
7 *Ibid.*, p. 18.
8 Thompson, *Taking Responsibility for the Past,* p. 36.
9 The UK citizenship test for potential citizens incorporates questions which require knowledge of the UK's national past and cultural values; see J. Löfström, 'Historical apologies as acts of symbolic inclusion – and exclusion? Reflections on institutional apologies as politics of cultural citizenship', *Citizenship Studies*, 15:1 (2011), 93–108, p. 97.
10 S. Mulhall and A. Swift, *Liberals and Communitarians* (Oxford: Blackwell, 2nd edn, 1996).
11 A. MacIntyre, *After Virtue: A Study In Moral Theory* (London: Duckworth, 2nd edn, 1985), pp. 220–1.
12 Smith, *I Was Wrong*, p. 202; Miller, *National Responsibility*, p. 142; M. Sandel, *Justice: What's The Right Thing To Do?* (London: Penguin, 2010), p. 222.
13 Miller, *National Responsibility*, pp. 140–1.
14 Sandel, *Justice*, p. 220.
15 This is discussed more fully in F. Abdel-Nour, 'National responsibility', *Political Theory*, 31:5 (2003), 693–719.
16 Celermajer, *The Sins of the Nation,* p. 184.
17 See G. Sher, 'Ancient wrongs and modern rights', *Philosophy and Public Affairs,* 10:1 (1981), 3–17; G. Sher, 'Transgenerational compensation', *Philosophy and Public Affairs*, 33:2 (2005), 181–200 and J. Waldron, 'Superseding historic injustice', *Ethics*, 103:1 (1992), 4–28 for a more detailed discussion.
18 Thompson, *Taking Responsibility for the Past*, p. 82.
19 Brooks, 'The New Patriotism and Apology for Slavery', 213–33 in Barkan and Karn (eds), *Taking Wrongs Seriously*, p. 225.
20 Cunningham; 'Saying sorry: the politics of apology'; R. Joyce, 'Apologizing', *Public Affairs Quarterly*, 13:2 (1999), 159–73, p. 164, emphasis in original.
21 Thaler, 'Just pretending', p. 271.
22 B. Anderson, *Imagined Communities: Reflections on the Origins and Spread of Nationalism* (London: Verso, 1993).
23 The traumatic view of the famine is found in B. Bradshaw, 'Nationalism and historical scholarship in modern Ireland', *Irish Historical Studies*, 26:104 (1989), 329–51.
24 See references in the section 'Slavery' in the bibliographical note.
25 Weyeneth, 'The power of apology and the process of historical reconciliation', pp. 19–20. See also Chapter 5.
26 T. Govier, *Forgiveness and Revenge* (London: Routledge, 2002), p. 89, emphasis in original.
27 There are limitations to this in practice. If as a white British person I saw myself as a recipient of an apology to indigenous Australians, others would judge me somewhat strange.
28 For the extent of political opposition, see figures cited in J. Torpey, 'Paying for the past?: The movement for reparations for African-Americans', *Journal of Human Rights*, 3:2 (2004), 171–87, p. 176. Pettigrove in 'Apology, reparations and the

question of inherited guilt', pp. 319–20; R. L. Brooks in 'Not Even an Apology?', 309–14 in Brooks (ed.), *When Sorry Isn't Enough*, p. 312 and Coicaud, 'Apology', pp. 115–16 argue that one reason Clinton opposed an apology was fear of lawsuits regarding compensation or reparation.

29 Logically, policies to tackle disadvantage can be adopted without any interest in, or knowledge of, the historical basis of such disadvantage.

30 See, for example, Tavuchis, *Mea Culpa* and, more recently, Lazare, *On Apology*; Thompson, 'Apology, Justice and Respect'; Smith, *I Was Wrong*; M. Mihai, 'When the state says "sorry": State apologies as exemplary political judgments', *Journal of Political Philosophy*, doi: 10.1111/j.1467-9760.2012.00418.x (April 2012, 1–21) and Thaler, 'Just pretending'.

31 *Ibid.*

32 These ideas are discussed by Nobles, *The Politics of Official Apologies.* In Northern Ireland, there have been extensive strategies for citizen inclusion for the nationalist community, though without a formal apology. Examples since the late 1960s include changes in political and institutional structures, electoral reform, policing reform, housing policy, fair employment legislation and the practices associated with 'parity of esteem' to recognise the validity of the cultural, linguistic and historical aspects of nationalist identity.

33 This will be considered further in Chapter 6.

34 This does not mean that every apology demanded or granted will be defended as justified.

35 For the British experience see M. Kenny, 'Taking the temperature of the political elite 2: the professionals move in?', *Parliamentary Affairs*, 62:2 (2009), 335–44; M. Kenny, 'Taking the temperature of the British political elite 3: when grubby is the order of the day …', *Parliamentary Affairs*, 62:3 (2009), 503–13; P. Riddell, 'In defence of politicians: in spite of themselves', *Parliamentary Affairs*, 63:3 (2010), 545–57 and R. Fox, 'Disgruntled, disillusioned and disengaged: public attitudes to politics in Britain today', *Parliamentary Affairs*, 65:4 (2012), 877–87. For a comparative perspective see P. Schmitter, 'Re-presenting representation' (Review article), *Government and Opposition*, 44: 4 (2009), 476–90, and N. Allen and S. Birch, 'Political conduct and misconduct: probing public opinion', *Parliamentary Affairs*, 64:1 (2011), 61–81.

4

The ideological location of the apology

In Chapter 2, the emergence of the apology was discussed and it was claimed that the apology could be supported by drawing on different political traditions. Both the universalist discourse of human rights and the more particularistic claims associated with communitarian thought can be drawn upon to underpin arguments in favour of the apology. In Chapter 3, four particular issues and problems associated with the political apology were identified. The purpose of this chapter is to further focus upon how the apology relates to different ideological traditions and whether, for example, they can be invoked to support or undermine the coherence of the idea of the apology. Despite the now extensive literature concerning the apology, there has been little systematic attempt to 'map' it against the dominant ideologies of American and European politics.

The ideological traditions: socialism, liberalism and conservatism

This section will 'map' the apology against three of the major ideological traditions of Western politics. Two preliminary points need to be made here. First, it is a banality to emphasise the diversity and complexities of these traditions; nonetheless it is possible to outline certain assumptions and 'ways of thinking' generally associated with the traditions which differentiate them and the compatibility of these with the apology.[1] Second, it is useful to construct reflections around these ideologies as they inform, implicitly or explicitly, both the way in which many political theorists think about justice and related concepts and the way in which political organisations and groupings respond in practice to the phenomenon of the apology in the public sphere.

The first ideological tradition to be considered is the socialist tradition. It will be argued that this tradition is broadly incompatible with the apology and would question the utility of the apology in politics. There are four elements of this tradition which either render the apology unsustainable or, at least, sit uneasily with it. These are its 'forward looking' orientation, its universalism, its materialism and the importance of class.

Historically, socialism (in its Marxist, social-democratic or utopian forms) was an ideology which was concerned with the construction of a new society born of the European Enlightenment faith in reason and progress and can thus be deemed 'forward looking'. For example, Schwarzmantel argues that utopian socialists as well as those in the Marxist tradition saw the productive potential of the industrial revolution as the possible basis for their emancipatory project.[2] Other commentators have contested this: for example, Vincent claims that socialism 'has accepted wholeheartedly *and* repudiated the role of Enlightenment rationalism'.[3] However, I would argue that the balance lies much more with the pro-Enlightenment elements and traditions of socialism.

Some commentators, including Torpey, consider that the rise of what he terms the reparation and 'historical injustice' movement, of which debates and mobilisations around apology can be considered a part, reflects the collapse of forward-looking political projects and a turn to the past. He states 'efforts to rectify past wrongs have … jostled with, and perhaps to some degree supplanted, expansive visions of an alternative human future of the kind that animated the socialist and civil rights movements of the preceding century'.[4] Therefore, the tendency to look back and to make history and memory central to the political project, as much academic and practical work associated with apology does, marks a retreat or turning away from the construction of the new society. It might be objected that apology can be conceived as, or considered as, a 'forward-looking' enterprise in that either the examination of history (and perhaps memory) is a necessary part of bringing about reconciliation between groups or that the recognition of previously marginalised groups is necessary for a just, future society.[5] If this is the case, then the apology might have a compatibility with the socialist tradition. However, it seems to me that these concerns are more associated with what might be termed post-socialist 'leftist' politics which has critiqued a more traditional socialism for its concentration on class and material inequality at the expense of other sources of inequality.

Second, and connected to the previous point, socialism is a tradition of universalism. Through revolution or state intervention or decentralising power, depending on the particular variant of the tradition, society could be recast for the benefit of all. This universalism is, potentially at least, challenged or breached by forms of politics which focus on difference. It may be argued that this is not necessarily true of the 'politics of apology'; however, as previously discussed, many cases do involve recognition of a group or community as different and may underpin a form of politics, or political arrangements and structures, which sit uneasily with universalism. This may occur within the state or polity; however (some of) socialism's traditional scepticism about, or hostility towards, nationalism is rooted in nationalism's undermining of universalism. Again, it may be objected that socialism is compatible with nationalism and clearly some historically existing socialist movements embraced nationalism, although the relationship between the two was often contentious.[6] However, in variants of socialism which stress (or stressed) internationalism or the class basis of organisation, nationalism was a potentially disruptive and reactionary ideology.

Third, socialism is a tradition rooted in the material. Various forms, including Marxism, much ethical socialism, social democracy and technocratic forms share a concern with the material, whether the focus is upon production, distribution or other concerns relating to work or labour. According to Freeden, 'all socialisms conceive of human nature as essentially productive ... and work or labour is seen as a major component of that natural activity'.[7] Although the apology may be linked to, or be the precursor to, material forms of compensation or reparation it can be conceptually and practically separate and thus the apology itself lies in the symbolic sphere of politics. There may be more than one socialist conceptualisation of justice but most are much more likely to favour a material-related conceptualisation related to collective ownership, reconstituted property relations or redistributive policies than to the arena of the symbolic. Some evidence to support this point may be adduced from the fact that various 'leftist' groups have been critical of apologies because they believe the focus on the symbolic, as they interpret it, is less important than material issues of compensation or reparation.

The fourth point about class relates to the question of intergenerational responsibility discussed in Chapter 3. Supporters of the apology often argue that it is meaningful for either the state or the nation to assume responsibility for events which preceded the existence of any current members of the state's institutions (e.g. the head of state, the prime minister, members of the legislature) or any of the people who currently constitute the nation.[8] To expand upon this point, let us consider the debate over whether Britain should apologise for its role in the transatlantic slave trade.[9] From a socialist perspective, a possible problem with the state or the nation taking collective responsibility which resonates over time is that this approach fails to focus sufficiently on the class dimension of power in two ways. One is that at the time of the slave trade the working class in Britain was disenfranchised and the British state was ruled by an oligarchy. This fact could be cited to undermine the attempt to make the British people collectively responsible for actions carried out in this period. The second and related point is that the immediate and direct beneficiaries of the trade were, disproportionately if not exclusively, merchants and plantation owners and not the British working class. Given that the wealth accrued from such a trade is massively skewed, why should all Britons be held collectively responsible rather than those who benefited the most?[10] In short, if the power which brought about injustice and the material benefits which accrued from the injustice are related to a specific class it is implausible to hold the entire nation responsible.

Liberalism is the second ideological tradition to be considered. It can be argued that important strands of the liberal tradition sit uneasily with the concept of apology. The liberal focus on the individual and individual autonomy, both ontologically and politically, renders the idea of collective responsibility problematic. This is particularly a problem if responsibility over generations is considered in national collective terms since much of liberalism would recoil at the idea that an autonomous individual could be held responsible for that which she had not done. If the focus is moved from the nation to the state having responsibility, it can be argued that the problem is reduced. This is because the institutional continuity of the state can allow, for example, a prime minister to apologise for something that preceded her birth because she apologises as an office-holder and not as an individual whose autonomy or sense of responsibility is compromised. By way of analogy, the liberal tradition does not deem the keeping of treaties, or offering recompense for their breaching, problematic because of its recognition of institutional continuity which is a characteristic of states and promotes *inter alia* a stable world order.

A second way in which an emphasis on individualism can make the apology problematic or incoherent is related to the indeterminacy question above. In many of the high-profile cases of apology, claimed or given, it is difficult to identify without controversy who are victims of injustice. The injustices associated with slavery and the treatment of aboriginal groupings stand as examples that include people, as members of collectives, who had radically different experiences and people who are far removed in time, space or circumstance from the worst or original injustice.[11] If the concept of justice, like that of responsibility, is closely connected to identifiable people suffering specific acts as in liberal juridical constructions, the indeterminacy of victims of injustice renders some apologies intellectually dubious.[12] That these 'wider' conceptualisations of justice are incompatible with liberalism chimes with Celermajer's claims that the rise of the apology since the 1980s is related to conceptualisations that have 'defied the logic of liberalism's justice'.[13]

A third objection from a liberal perspective is one of universalism. Although constructed differently, liberalism shares socialism's universalistic claims and some apologies, though by no means all, may run counter to these claims. If the apology is related to a recognition of difference, or a difference that can undermine or challenge the idea of universal citizenship and be used to claim differential treatment or constitutional arrangements, it breaches the notion of universalism which is a strong component of the liberal tradition.

Thus, again, as with the examples of socialist ideology, it can be conceded that this 'fits' better older manifestations and forms of liberalism than more contemporary developments. Some liberal thinkers have argued for exceptions to universalism in certain laws or procedures to protect minority groups which run counter to conceptualisations that emphasise procedural equality.[14]

Fourth, there is the question of time. As Weiner has observed, what constitutes time or a 'long time' differs in different spheres of human activity and the frameworks associated with them.[15] If liberal theories of justice are linked to individual responsibility, the identification of those wronged and concepts of property and rectification associated with a Western tradition of jurisprudence, these concepts are often linked to evidence or procedures that are time-limited. They may be unwilling or unable to recognise claims of injustice which exist in spheres employing a theological or therapeutic framework in which time is differently constructed.

Of the three major ideological traditions considered, the conservative one is most compatible with the concept of the apology and its intellectual integrity. This is particularly the case when the apology involved depends upon the idea of collective responsibility and the recipients of the apology being a collective, rather than clearly identifiable individuals. Unlike liberalism, an important strand in conservative thinking gives ontological priority to the collective or communal over the individual and places more emphasis on the individual being constituted by, and rooted in, a communal sense of identity. As with the other traditions above, it can be argued that there are countervailing tendencies since there is a strong tendency in contemporary conservatism that emphasises individualism; although a counter to this objection is that this is part of an adoption and adaption of liberal concerns by contemporary conservative movements and parties.

A second and related point is that history is central to conservative conceptualisations of what a society is and how the current individuals and subjects in it understand themselves. Therefore, if the apology (and often related forms of reparation) is part of a 'backward-looking' form of politics and that the framework of time involved is one which can encompass several generations, this is compatible with a conservative way of thinking. This is important because often those communities or collectives seeking the apology argue that the effects of the original injustice shape the experiences and collective consciousness of successive generations. This conceptualisation of how individuals are constituted, e.g. with the history and memory of their community, underpins the argument that these effects have a contemporary resonance. From this perspective, it is possible to critique the 'narrowness' of a liberal conception of justice which focuses upon legal redress and is often premised on individual or corporate responsibility and the identification of specific individuals as victims of the injustice.

Beyond the ideological traditions: some reflections on the practical politics of apology

It is argued here that the two traditions of socialism and liberalism, or important variants of them, are incompatible with certain types of apology and that the conservative tradition is broadly compatible with the apology. However, the popular political discourse around apology does not seem to match the ideological landscape. By this is meant that, as a generalisation, the writers, newspapers, pressure groups and organisations which support or defend the apology come from the liberal left while those which tend to be sceptical or hostile can be located on the political right. This may appear to be something of a contradiction, even if one cannot expect common political discourse or forms of mobilisation to fit neatly with ideological or theoretical traditions. However, this disjuncture can be explained.

Why do those of a liberal left disposition tend to support the apology? The rise of the apology in the public sphere, and campaigns associated with it, has roughly coincided with an emergence, or revival, in political theory of a concern about how, and in what ways, historically excluded or marginalised groups can contest their disadvantaged status. This body of work includes much that can be subsumed under the terms 'the politics of difference' or 'the politics of recognition'.[16] While this work is by no means *necessarily* associated with the liberal left, it has proved useful and been adopted by many with this disposition in the realm of political activism. For those with sympathy for groups whose history as a collective (based on ethnic or other forms of exclusion) has been marginalised, distorted or ignored, the apology may be one way in which this exclusion can be addressed. (Contingently, the apology may be linked to forms of reparation, restitution or affirmative action.) Therefore, it is not surprising that the liberal left may regard the apology as defensible as it is part of a politics of support for the less powerful in society, either domestically or globally.

An impetus to this form of politics is that many theorists hold inadequate the more traditional forms of liberalism or socialism to address these concerns. Liberalism's conceptualisation of universalism and individualism could neither present an adequate account of how individuals are constituted nor justify the forms of political structures and arrangements necessary to recognise or acknowledge difference. Socialism shared with liberalism the universalism which has been critiqued and the emphasis on the material within this tradition outlined above has failed in two ways. First, this tradition failed to emphasise sufficiently the importance of the non-material in the satisfaction of human need, for example the need for recognition and, second, the failure of existing socialist states and the rise of neo-liberalism undermined a faith in the practicality of wholesale structural reform of economic organisation or even the viability of redistributive policies. Obviously, not all theorists have abandoned liberalism or socialism but many writers who can be considered 'leftist' in orientation have argued that these traditions have proved inadequate in their conceptualisations of justice and their treatment of marginalised groupings or communities.

It will now be considered why the 'right', or political conservatives, tend to be hostile towards the apology. There are two principal reasons although I think the second is more fundamental. First, there is the concern that the apology is, or can be, related to claims for particular arrangements which have a claim on the public purse and are examples of 'special pleading' by particularistic interest groups.[17] This is particularly a concern for the strand of conservatism that draws upon a neo-liberal distaste for public expenditure or that which considers pluralistic pressures as 'overloading' government or diverting it from the national interest. Second, the apology is often related to challenging the dominant narrative of the nation's history or impugning that history. This challenge is found in both cases of intra-state apology and inter-state apology. The nation's history and its representation is important in popular conservative discourse so challenges are often seen as illegitimate or pernicious in that they undermine what might be termed the 'traditional' collective view of the nation. There are numerous examples of conservative groupings who oppose apologies on these grounds, either to groupings within the nation or to other nations.[18]

If correct, these claims indicate that the politics of apology emerge in the context of, and are underpinned by, a broadly communitarian political ideology and specific campaigns for apology are more likely to be supported by those of a leftist disposition. To this extent, the apology is located ideologically and historically in a period where the ideological focus on universalism and progress has been challenged by the emergence, or re-emergence, of the importance of the particular and of history.

In conclusion a cautionary note should be posted about trying to fit the discourse around apology neatly into ideological 'camps'. In this chapter it has been argued that individuals or collectives make a claim for apology on the basis of an injustice having being committed. Given these claims are often made against other nations/states and across time, there is often an implication from those claiming an apology or their advocates that some consensus may be reached on what constitutes an injustice or how it may be defined. If the search for a definition for injustice is to go beyond the temporally or socially specific, the search would seem to be moving toward a universal standard of how an act can be evaluated in terms of its just or unjust status.[19] If this is the case, then the basis of the claim for apology (an injustice committed) is invoking the language and tradition of universalism while the realisation of the apology often depends upon the invocation of constructions of responsibility and temporality that draw heavily upon a communitarian tradition in opposition to such universality.

These considerations point to the possibility that the apology, and particular understandings of its meaning, defences of its utility or criticisms of its value, draw on three traditions which can be labelled pre-modern, modern and post-modern. An example of the first can be found in the work of Celermajer who links the rise of the apology with religious traditions of communal repentance and, as noted above (see p. 25), connects this to liberalism's inadequacies. She says: 'if we look within the sphere of secular politics itself, we simply will not find the historical roots or the background grammar for apology. By contrast, in the sphere of religion we find those missing tropes and the grammars we need to decode the contemporary practice.'[20] The individualism, 'rational' politics and limited conceptualisation of justice of modernist politics cannot account for the phenomenon of the apology. As discussed in Chapter 2, there is also a modernist discourse around universal rights and their extension that can, and is, used both to explain the rise of the apology and to justify the apology. There are two aspects to what may be termed the 'post-modern' discourse around apologies. One has been discussed already and would cover the writers who believe that the rise of the apology is linked to identity politics and the 'politics of difference' which, in turn, reflect the decline of industrial class-based politics of the modernist era and the inadequacy of liberal universalism to deal with long-established grievances or distorted identities. Logically, this retreat of modernism, for want of a better phrase, could be seen as a positive or negative development; however many writers on the apology who relate it to this development are broadly supportive of it.

A more critical position is taken by those who associate the apology with trends in politics in which, in this account, individual and collective emotions have entered the public sphere and 'rational' politics has been dethroned. One example of this can be found in *The Tyranny of Guilt* by political commentator and essayist Pascal Bruckner.[21] Bruckner berates western nations for indulging in guilt about past crimes and injustices rather than emphasising the dualism of past vice and virtue in the history of the 'West' and addressing the injustices of the contemporary period. In doing this, there is a flight from defending liberty, democracy and rights which are associated with the Enlightenment and modernism. This politics is specifically linked to the apology in one passage: 'there comes a time when moral and metaphysical culpability is used to elude [*sic*] any real political responsibility. The debt to the dead wins out over the duty to the living. *Repentance creates people who apologize for ancient crimes in order to exonerate themselves for present crimes.*'[22]

It is an interesting aspect of the apology that it can be interpreted in many ways and draw upon different traditions; as the welcome manifestation of a communal, religiously inspired repentance, as the recognition and extension of universal rights or as an example of inappropriate and self-indulgent emotion as the politics of reason and a defence of Enlightenment values are usurped. These three versions can be seen as examples of pre-modern, modern and post-modern resonances in reflections on the apology.

Notes

1 All the main introductory texts on ideologies stress the various strands within the different ideological traditions and the diversity within them.
2 J. Schwarzmantel, *The Age of Ideology: Political Ideologies from The American Revolution to Postmodern Times* (Basingstoke, Macmillan, 1998), p. 88.
3 A. Vincent, *Modern Political Ideologies* (Oxford: Blackwell, 2nd edn, 1995), p. 91 (emphasis in original).
4 Torpey, 'An Avalanche of History', p. 28.
5 For more on the concept of recognition see Chapter 7.
6 One historical example is the divergent attitudes of European socialists to the outbreak of the First World War.
7 M. Freeden, *Ideologies and Political Theory: A Conceptual Approach* (Oxford: Clarendon Press, 1996), p. 429.
8 See the discussion in the first section of Chapter 3.
9 See Cunningham, '"It wasn't us and we didn't benefit"'.
10 *Ibid.*, pp. 254–5.
11 German reparation paid to Israel after the Second World War benefited some Israeli citizens who had not been involved in the Holocaust.
12 As indicated in the discussion in Chapter 3, some apologies involve easily identifiable victims; some do not.
13 Celermajer, *The Sins of the Nation*, p. 2.
14 Will Kymlicka is one example. He argues that special arrangements or practices to defend minority cultures do not breach liberal principles.
15 Weiner, *The Sins of the Parents*, pp. 19–23.
16 See also the discussion of Charles Taylor and Axel Honneth in Chapter 7.
17 These criticisms are found in the context of African American and indigenous Australian claims; for more details see Chapter 5.
18 Germany, Japan, France, Israel, the United Kingdom, the USA and Australia are just a few examples of countries where, in recent years, conservative elements have protested about attacks on the nation's history or historical narratives.
19 The codification of Human Rights after the Second World War marks an attempt to establish minimum universal standards (see also Chapter 2).
20 Celermajer, *The Sins of the Nation*, p. 8.
21 P. Bruckner, *The Tyranny of Guilt: An Essay on Western Masochism* (Princeton, NJ: Princeton University Press, 2010).
22 *Ibid.*, p. 98 (emphasis in original).

5

Intra-state apologies: reflections on the politics of support and opposition

Introduction

This chapter builds on the ideas outlined in Chapter 3 about the issues of responsibility, time, indeterminacy and sincerity and the ideological location of the apology discussed in Chapter 4. The purpose is to try to think further about why people may, or may not, support particular apologies and which factors and variables influence these positions. The nature of this chapter will be somewhat discursive and speculative. However, it is hoped that it offers a way to think about political responses to the apology. The focus will be on intra-state apologies as aspects of inter-state apologies will be considered in Chapter 6.

It is useful to begin with an outline of some of the methodological difficulties in trying to establish what citizens of any particular country think about a specific apology, or about the process of partial, incomplete or successive apologies. While some quantitative material is available, it is patchy and incomplete so it is difficult to state precisely what proportion of citizens are broadly supportive of, or hostile to, the apology. It is plausible that many citizens have no strong opinions about the topic given that there is evidence that in most liberal democracies engagement with politics and forms of political participation is relatively low.[1]

If it is difficult to gauge precisely levels of support for the apology, the qualitative issues throw up greater problems still. The simple question of why people support/oppose the apology is fraught with complexities which will be set out here. A trawl of websites, blogs and letters pages of newspapers provides some indication of attitudes towards the apology; however clearly it is a self-selecting group which contributes to such forums. It is difficult to make estimates of how representative these particular contributions are, however they can be useful in providing a 'snapshot' of the political discourse around the apology and some will be employed later in the chapter. Along with issues of quantification and representativeness, a third potential problem emerges which is that of the citizen's understanding and interpretation of the apology. In other words, if one can establish, for example, how many people support a specific apology and on what grounds, this does not necessarily tell one anything of the different understandings that may be brought to bear about the intention or purpose of the apology. This will be illustrated with some hypothetical examples. USA citizen A supports, in principle, an apology for slavery because she believes or hopes that the symbolism of the apology will provide a degree of acknowledgement or recognition of the injustice suffered by African-American citizens which will satisfy their demand for redress as a collective and thus reduce the group's claims for reparation which she believes is an unreasonable burden on the American taxpayer. Citizen B supports the apology because he believes that the granting of the apology as an acknowledgement of the past injustice of slavery will help to underpin the case for reparations which are needed as a material response to past injustice. Citizen C opposes the apology because it will be used by others or the government to deflect from the need to pay reparations. Citizen D opposes the apology because current citizens have no responsibility to rectify an injustice that preceded their existence and, anyway, those wanting one are engaged in unjustified 'special pleading'. Citizen E supports an apology because she feels ashamed about America's history of slavery; Citizen F believes the emotion of shame is irrelevant to the political apology but supports an apology because he accepts the concept of intergenerational responsibility.

These examples could be multiplied. However, the ones provided are intended to illustrate the simple, but fundamental, point that there are potentially many different readings, interpretations and understandings of what the apology means. In certain cases, the apology is a particular statement or text which can be deconstructed; this will not, of course, guarantee a consensus about meaning as all texts have to be interpreted. The potential for very different readings and understandings of the apology is increased and exacerbated by two other factors. First, in some circumstances, there is not one, or only one, 'actual' or 'real' apology which can be argued over in terms of meaning; there is a series of statements, speeches, sometimes by different actors or institutions, which comprise a diversity of partial, semi- or qualified apologies.[2] Therefore, some notion of what the apology 'really means', if not in any case a chimera, becomes even more obscure and opaque. Second, as discussed in Chapter 1, the discussion about, and understanding of, the apology in politics are difficult to decouple from the legacy of the personal apology. If this connection percolates into the popular discourse, it adds another layer of contention or imprecision about what endorsing, or not endorsing, an apology means. The most obvious way in which this resonates is in relation to emotion. For example, there are those who resist the apology because they feel no shame, guilt or regret about the injustice under consideration; however this position is irrelevant and arguably misguided for those who advocate the decoupling of the adoption of personal dispositions and emotions from association with the political apology. To summarise, the whole discourse about apology becomes 'muddy' and contested because all statements and expressions can be interpreted in different ways, but also because apologies sometimes constitute a 'process' rather than a 'one-off' statement and the pertinence and applicability of the emotions adds a dimension that is not unique to the apology in public discourse but one that is writ large.

Bearing in mind these complexities, some thoughts will be offered about why people support or oppose apologies. One way to think about this topic is to consider the articulation of the political context of specific apologies with the themes addressed in Chapter 3 which can be invoked and articulated for or against the apology. This duality is an attempt to indicate that citizens' political responses can reflect and invoke more abstract themes (as in Chapter 3) but will articulate them within political contexts which can influence and shape them. It would need further empirical testing to see how well this duality would fit or help to map attitudes in all cases of apology; this chapter will consider apologies relating to three case studies of slavery in the USA, the aboriginal experience in Australia and the apology for Bloody Sunday in the UK. With respect to the first two examples, specific attention will be given to the Senate apology of 2009 and the Rudd apology of 2008 since they are chronologically close to each other and both are close to the Bloody Sunday apology of 2010. The justification for this selection is partly pragmatic in relation to access to Anglophone sources and partly because the three cases have commonalities in that the concept of 'insider' and 'outsider' groups are pertinent to all but there are also significant differences.[3] For ease of comparison, the case studies will have four sections. The first is the chronology to give some sense of the timeframe of apology discourse, the second covers opinion poll material on support or opposition to the apology, the third considers the political context and how this informs the debate and the fourth provides some examples of the discourse from public and politicians.

Slavery in the USA

Chronology

Since 1989, Democrat Representative John Conyers has annually drafted a bill to set up a commission to study the impact of slavery and the issue of reparations. However, the bill has made no progress and does not seem to have generated much public attention. Further developments date from the mid to late 1990s with President Clinton's 'dialogue on race' and the introduction by a Democrat Representative, Tony Hall, of a resolution in the House of Representatives in 1997 apologising for slavery. However, the impact of these was limited as the resolution had no legislative implications and President Clinton refused to endorse the apology or make a formal presidential statement of apology.[4] In March 1998, while in Uganda as part of a longer tour of Africa, Clinton expressed what has been described as 'regret and contrition' for slavery; however, as recorded earlier, various commentators attribute his reluctance to make a more formal statement including an IFID of 'apology' because of its possible connection to reparation claims. The political divisiveness of the issue has also been alluded to by some commentators.[5] The limited nature of the statement is also captured in Barkan's description of it as an 'unplanned semiapology'.[6] In July 2003, on a visit to Senegal in West Africa, Clinton's successor as president, George W. Bush also expressed regret about slavery without issuing an apology in that there was no recognition of responsibility. One commentator has described it as a 'near apology' and ascribes the reluctance to apologise as fear of the unknown in respect of what might happen next. Interestingly, the question of 'what happens after the apology' is asked rhetorically.[7] One might infer that a major issue is that of reparations, since the prospect of reparation following the apology, or being decoupled from it, has the potential to antagonise different political constituencies within the USA.

The two most recent developments at the level of national politics are an apology by the House of Representatives in July 2008 and one by the Senate in June 2009. Three initial observations are worth making here about the latter apology. First, like Hall's resolution of 1997 and the House resolution of 2008, it had bipartisan support. Second, unlike both it had a specific disclaimer which noted that nothing in the resolution: '(A) authorizes or supports any claim against the United States; or (B) serves as a settlement of any claim against the United States.'[8] Once again the promise or threat of reparations looms over the debate. Third, the resolution also includes an apology for wrongs committed under Jim Crow laws. This is significant inasmuch that objections to an apology for slavery may be constructed on different grounds to that of Jim Crow laws; this will be highlighted below in the discussion of time and consequence. As well as the Congressional resolution, the increasing traction of the apology is indicated in that, by 2009, eight states had apologised for slavery: Alabama, Arkansas, Florida, Maryland, North Carolina, Virginia, New Jersey and Connecticut and others have been considering an apology.

Opinion polls

The above section is not intended to provide an exhaustive narrative of developments but to provide a brief chronological context for the subsequent reflections. The second section will provide some quantitative material about attitudes towards the apology for slavery. A 1997 poll revealed that two-thirds of African-Americans supported an apology and compensation and two-thirds of whites opposed an apology and 88 per cent opposed reparation. A poll of 2000 indicated that 70 per cent of whites supported an apology and 30 per cent opposed, while among African-Americans 79 per cent supported an apology and 21 per cent were opposed. A 2002 poll found that 80 per cent of African-Americans wanted an apology and 69 per cent wanted reparations, while 30 per cent of whites supported an apology and only 4 per cent supported monetary compensation. Another poll of 2002, commissioned by CNN/USA Today, showed that 90 per cent of white American opposed reparations while more than half of African-Americans supported them. A poll of 2008 indicated that 53 per cent of white Americans opposed a federal apology.[9] Allowing for the possibility of sampling errors or factors such as the terms compensation or reparation not being precisely defined, there is a clear picture of a racial divide in broad or general terms in relation to the apology for slavery.

Political context

The next section will consider the political context of the apology. The intention is to try to outline what seem to be the most significant factors in affecting how contributors to the debate understand the apology and what meaning they give to it. Or, to put it another way, what frames the debate and dialogue being held. These factors will then be put alongside the more abstract ideas which were the subject of Chapter 3. Looking at the apology for slavery in the USA, three factors are of particular significance. One is the racialised nature of American politics, or more specifically how attitudes to the apology, and in particular to reparation, correlate with racial groupings.[10] (It should be emphasised here that race is not being used in some biologically essentialist way but as a basis of political mobilisation or form of identity which is mutable, fluid and potentially overlain and undermined by other multiple forms of identity.) The second, and related, factor is the context of the reparations issue; this is an older debate than the one surrounding apology and has generated an extensive literature.[11] The salient point is that, although they are logically and conceptually different, in practice the apology and reparation have become largely entwined so much of the discussion and debate reflects this. So, for example, some oppose the apology because it may be the 'slippery slope' to reparation, some support it because it may herald the sought-for and desired reparation. Some supporters of the apology would see it as good but inadequate with reparation being the test of the sincerity of the apology. The simple point here is that one cannot read the academic material, the congressional statements or the blogs about apology without reparation casting its contextual shadow.

The third factor is that attitudes to the apology are influenced by understandings of the contemporary situation of the African-American population. There are potentially multiple versions of these understandings and they will not 'neatly' follow racial lines. However, it is my contention that these understandings, like reparation, are politically enmeshed or intertwined with the way the apology is thought about. Some bloggers, especially conservative ones, either deny the existence of patterns of African-American socio-economic disadvantage or accept that these patterns exist but are not linked to the legacy of slavery. The holders of such views are unlikely to be supporters of an apology for slavery (though some could be); not because slavery was justified but because the contemporary apology campaign is identified with a 'way of understanding' and a political worldview to which they are hostile.[12] Another way in which opposition to the apology is articulated is by arguing that it is irrelevant or redundant because the American Civil War and the trajectory of American politics since mark a *de facto* apology in that the blood shed by unionists at the Civil War battles, civil rights legislation, affirmative action or some combination of these constitute atonement for the stain of slavery.

Before looking at some concrete examples, it is worth speculating on how the 'racialisation' of the issue can impact. Some white voters and contributors to the debate, although it would be difficult if not impossible to quantify how many in this context and others, may think in group terms based on racial identity. What this entails can be precisely defined; what is postulated here is that there are those who do not feel an affective connection to their fellow citizens because of (constructed or perceived) racial difference. This may manifest itself in overt hostility to the 'other' in racist language and actions or it may be a more diffuse indifference to the political concerns, identity or culture of the 'other'. The question here, which is largely rhetorical, is the plausibility that what may seem to be more principled objections to an apology may be used as a rationalisation for more sectarian or exclusionist sentiments, particularly if the latter are difficult to express overtly because they are politically 'beyond the pale'. To expand, does the critique of the apology based, for example, on the responsibility or time issues discussed in Chapter 3, here termed 'principled' because they do not serve a partisan purpose, act in practice to mask a more narrowly 'political' opposition? A hypothetical example will help to illustrate this. If a group of white Americans had experienced an injustice comparable to slavery, with the same issues of current American citizens not being directly responsible (responsibility), the injustice being formally ended in the mid-nineteenth century (time) and a controversy over identifying the precise victims (indeterminacy), would these issues still be as salient in constructing a critique of the apology? Or, as seems more plausible, would there be much more support for the apology because the victims were part of the same group, with which there were strong affective ties? This is not to claim that all objections to the apology in the USA context based on these three issues (responsibility, time, indeterminacy) are 'simply' racist, partly because some are held by African-Americans. The point is that particular critiques may be used to bolster positions that are largely determined by the politics of group membership in the context of 'insider' and 'outsider' groups.

Here we return to a further discussion about the Senate apology of 2009, the most recent institutional apology at national level. As indicated above, both the context of reparation and the legacy of Jim Crow laws inform the text of the resolution and four more extracts will be highlighted which give some indication of the audience and context of the piece. First, there is a clear emphasis on the connections between slavery, later practices of discrimination and their effects. For example: 'African-Americans continue to suffer from the consequences of slavery and Jim Crow laws – long after both systems were formally abolished – through enormous damage and loss, both tangible and intangible, including the loss of human dignity and liberty.'[13] This extract and earlier sections can be interpreted as 'heading off' the criticisms and objections that 'it was all a long time ago' and also the word 'intangible' can be interpreted as an endorsement of the idea that psychological or other non-material damage still resonates. The apology also states that enslavement and segregation 'should not be purged from or minimized in the telling of the history of the United States'.[14] This can be read as an admonition to those who criticise the interrogation of a nation's past and has parallels with the 'black armband' view of history debate in Australia. It is also claimed that the apology 'can speed racial healing and reconciliation'; thus the apology is not (only) 'backward-looking' but has a forward-looking dynamic in improving race relations within the USA.[15] The resolution concludes: 'it is important for the people of the United States, who legally recognized slavery through the Constitution and the laws of the United States, to make a formal apology for slavery and its successor, Jim Crow, so they can move forward and seek reconciliation, justice and harmony for all people of the United States'.[16] Two points should be noted here: the apology is being made in the name of the people, although it is far from clear that a majority of the people did endorse it. It may be that the Senate felt the apology had a greater moral force if in the name of the people and the positive benefits of the apology redound to all Americans; hence the 'special pleading' or divisive nature of the apology which is claimed by some of its critics is rebuffed.

In summary, the text of the resolution aimed to undermine some of the criticisms of the apology which have been articulated around issues of time, effect and that of sectarianism. The message one can take from the text is that, as injustices still resonate and their recognition would benefit all Americans, the apology should be endorsed.

Discourse

How this resonated with the American public can be illustrated through a review of some of the comments logged in a discussion board about the Senate resolution.[17] As indicated already, this is only a 'snapshot' of the debate and does not indicate the numbers in particular camps; however it gives a flavour of positions adopted at a popular level. The following listed comments constitute the main areas of contention and offer a brief commentary (noted in parentheses).

1 Reparations: as justified: 'we are ENTITLED to a formal apology and NOW definitely REPARATIONS to stem the tide of the "Living Consequences"' [capitals in original]. As unjustified: 'it annoys me when people look for an excuse for a handout'.

(This is part of a longer, heated discussion about the justification for, and impact of, affirmative action.)

2 Responsibility: denial of: 'This is just insulting that anybody alive today feels that we need to apologize for slavery. Nobody alive today in America is a slave; nobody alive today in America is a slave owner.'
'Being sorry and apologizing for what had been done by people that have died long before I was born just seems silly.'
Support for? (rhetorical): 'What constitutes "ownership" of a democratic political institution, like Congress or the national government? Is the US under new ownership since the days of slavery, or does the nation (or "the American people") have an existence which transcends any individual's lifetime?'

(See Chapter 3 to put this in context.)

3 'Always wanting more': 'The main reason I am against the apology is that I believe the issue will not be dropped there. There will some other thing to jump on in the name of black fairness.'
4 'Backward looking': 'Wake up America a Black Man is president, the future is here stop living in the past.'
5 'Attack on history': 'I guess we are not allowed to have a strong country anymore though. We have to apologize for everything we have ever done

... sorry for having black slaves (even though blacks were purchased from other black kings).'

6 (In response to 5 about 'black kings'.) 'Are you actually suggesting that we shouldn't be sorry, or shouldn't bother saying so, because OTHER PEOPLE also committed misdeeds? I hate to go back to how we raise children, but I seem to recall something about "two wrongs don't make a right"'.

The exchanges considered, and others posted on the discussion board, are a mixture of the visceral and intemperate and the reasoned and nuanced. What does emerge is that the perception of the current situation of African-Americans is crucial to the debate and there is a serious and informed discussion about the issue of responsibility by institutions and peoples over generations; one of the issues highlighted in Chapter 3. The issue of time seems less pertinent because of the linking of the debate on slavery to that of Jim Crow. The final three points are a little intemperate and ill-constructed but flag up popular responses experienced in other contexts.[18] These are: that apologies are backward-looking when the focus should be on the future, that they involve an unwarranted attack on the country's history and that apologies should not be given when others have committed injustices for which they have not apologised.

Apologies in Australia to the indigenous population

Chronology

The timeframe of the discussion about an apology in Australia for the treatment of the indigenous people roughly matches the American debate. In December 1992, Prime Minister Paul Keating made a speech, known as the 'Redfern Address' after the location of its delivery in Sydney, concerning the history of discrimination against aboriginal peoples. It is interesting to note that this speech illustrates well some of the definitional and interpretative issues around the apology raised in Chapter 1. Celermajer, who cites the speech at length, argues that it was 'in a sense, the first or proto-apology' and set the context for future discussion.[19] Thompson argues that it was not a political apology because Keating was not formally speaking as Prime Minister but expressing his opinion or that of his party and also on the grounds that it was not presented to indigenous Australians acting in a capacity as representatives of their people.[20]

The subsequent debate is largely framed by the Human Rights and Equal Opportunity Commission (HREOC) report, the short title of which was *Bringing Them Home*, published in 1997 about the forcible removal of indigenous children from their parents. This had a massive impact in Australian society; according to Augoustinos and LeCouteur it 'generated unprecedented public debate' and they claim that 'it is hard to imagine that any Australian could have remained untouched by this issue, or would not have been involved in the debate at some level over the past several years'.[21] The impact is also attested to by Attwood.[22] The HREOC inquiry had been established by a Labour government in 1995; however in 1996 John Howard, leader of the Liberal party, became Prime Minister in a Liberal-National party coalition and he did not endorse an apology. He expressed personal sorrow for injustices suffered, in the formulation he used in May 1997 at the opening of the Reconciliation Convention set up to consider the report; however he was not prepared to entertain the notion of institutional responsibility by the current Australian state. As has been discussed and critiqued in many texts, Howard associated such a position with the 'black armband' view of history which focused excessively, in his view, on the negative aspects of Australia's past.

In February 2008, the Labour Prime Minister Kevin Rudd, as one of the first actions of his newly elected government, issued a formal apology; 'formal' in that it contained the criteria that many commentators argue make a complete apology. This will not be discussed at length here as some of the salient points about the 'quality' and 'completeness' of Rudd's speech were considered in Chapter 1 and it has been examined in detail elsewhere.[23] The main point to emphasise here is the difference between the positions of Howard and Rudd. How this relates to the question of reconciliation will be considered further (see pp. 79–80). Rudd's apology was the last major one relating specifically to indigenous Australians, although in November 2009 he gave a national apology to 'Forgotten Australians' which included migrant children from the UK who had suffered various forms of abuse.

Opinion polls

Having sketched the chronology of apology in Australia, the next section provides some quantitative data about support for, and opposition to, the idea of apology or to specific apologies. According to Augoustinos and LeCouteur, Howard claimed his opposition to the formal apology, the position he adopted in 1997, reflected the views of a majority of citizens. However, they claim that some opinion polls indicated an even split among Australians on the issue, but they do not cite the polls themselves. They cite a different poll which found only 27 per cent of Perth residents supported a public apology.[24] Nobles cites a poll taken immediately after the HREOC report in which 65 per cent of Australians polled agreed with an apology; by 1999 a majority of 57 per cent was found to be against the idea, with 40 per cent supportive.[25] A BBC website at the time of Rudd's apology cited polls suggesting that roughly 30 per cent of Australians supported Howard's position; however there does not appear to be wholly convincing data available.[26] With reference to Howard, Weyeneth notes (in a footnote) that 'polls indicate that the prime minister enjoys strong popular support for his position, based to some extent on concern that an apology could open the door to compensation claims'.[27] However, no detail is given of these polls. Also as a footnote, Celermajer states that comprehensive polls on support for Howard's position were not conducted.[28]

There is some evidence that the apology has increasing support in recent years. One poll concerning attitudes towards the Rudd apology recorded the following figures for different categories: 44 per cent 'strongly support', 25 per cent 'somewhat support', 26 per cent 'not support' and 5 per cent 'uncommitted'.[29] Some commentaries, though lacking statistical detail, seem to bear out these attitudes. Burridge offers: 'the apology resonated with renewed spirit of unity amongst many Australians. While some disagreed and aired their disapproval on talkback radio, the majority of people agreed that it was a positive action.'[30] Similarly, Smith records the popular reception of the Rudd apology: 'the apology received tremendous support. The apology was not "merely" symbolic but has been accepted with relief, pride, gratitude and pleasure' and 'the reaction to the apology makes it clear that most Australians wanted to be associated with the apology.'[31]

Political context

Having briefly reviewed the chronology of the apology debate and the less-than-comprehensive quantitative data, the third theme is the political context of the apology, or rather the 'proto-apology', of Keating through Howard's oppositional stance to Rudd's official apology of 2008. It is instructive to compare this with the American case study above and try to highlight commonalities and differences. It is difficult to give a definitive list of the contextual factors in the debates; rather an attempt is made to point to some of the principal factors that frame the debate. As with the USA, there are two groups which could be designated as 'insider' and 'outsider', respectively white Australians and the Indigenous population. (These are the politically salient groups in the context of the debate; this designation is not meant to imply that every single Australian could be categorised thus or that identities are immutable.) Also, the issue of reparation acts as a 'backdrop' to the debate in Australia. Again, this can act on the debate in various ways and is comparable with the USA in that some white Australians have opposed the apology because of the suspicion that it will be part of a process fuelling reparation claims or will be used as a pretext. Nobles records that this was claimed by Howard, despite the fact that disclaimers could ensure there was not a legal basis.[32] Conversely, some indigenous activists and their supporters have expressed concern that the apology process, even in Rudd's formulation, is an unacceptable substitute for material reparation. Having said this, it seems, though this is impressionistic and hard to measure, that reparation is of greater significance in the US context because it has a greater centrality to the articulation of African-American grievances compared with the Australian case and because the relative sizes of the two communities means the financial implications of reparation would seem to be of a different magnitude.[33] (This, of course, depends on the way any reparation claims would be calculated.)

The question of 'insider' and 'outsider' groups will be considered here. While this acts as a point of comparison between the two cases in that racism and/or a lack of political sympathy and affective linkages to the 'other' play a part in attitudes, the two 'outsider' groups are different in that the closer parallel to indigenous Australians, in one way if not others, is Native Americans. This has two possible implications. One is whether the fact of the indigenous nature of the group has any bearing on the perceived legitimacy of the claims in the eyes of the 'insider' group; i.e. that their status as the original inhabitants of the country gives a moral force that is seen to be lacking in the claims of fellow citizens, as in the African-American case. The second implication is that the difference between the history of the Indigenous Australians and African-Americans impacts upon what reconciliation 'looks like' or what made be needed to achieve it between the two groups.

As will be discussed further in Chapter 7, reconciliation is often, implicitly or explicitly, linked to the apology; however reconciliation is often difficult to define or takes different forms. The Australian case is a good example of this, as Burridge demonstrates. She develops a threefold typology of reconciliation.[34] The first type is 'rights based' and variously described as 'hard', 'genuine', 'true' or 'substantive' and relates to rights indigenous peoples claim connected, for example, to native title, customary law and compensation for previous acts of dispossession. In essence, these are claims related to a different identity or sense of nationhood held by indigenous Australians. The second type is 'symbolic' and includes marches, ceremonies and gatherings. The third type is labelled 'assimilationist' and includes the 'practical' forms of reform that Howard focused upon, e.g. housing and education, that stress the 'sameness' of Australians. Citing an earlier study of the concept, Burridge states: 'to the more conservative elements in mainstream Australia, reconciliation is about equality and assimilation rather than Aboriginal peoples possessing distinct political and cultural rights'.[35]

This variety in the forms and meanings of reconciliation has two implications which make more difficult the process of analysis. First, it raises again the question introduced above about what people understand about the apology and its connection to other processes or policies. For example, it is logically possible for an Australian citizen to support 'type 2' reconciliation[36] in the hope that it will preclude the need for either public expenditure with 'type 3' reforms or the recognition of difference that 'type 1' implies. Alternatively, as noted, conservatives like Howard may be hostile to the politics underpinning, and the implications of, the first two types of reconciliation. Yet again, a combination of all three types of reconciliation may be deemed necessary by some to realise fully the political, cultural and socio-economic rights of indigenous peoples. More examples could be given of a hypothetical nature; however these illustrate the point that attitudes to any specific apology may be informed both by what is understood by the apology and how it articulates with associated processes like reconciliation. When what is meant by reconciliation is complex and contestable, the variety of interpretations and political positions is likely to be greater still.

The second point relates to the difference between the US and Australian examples used here. The commonalities are that both of the 'outsider' groups suffered from legally enshrined discrimination which impacted negatively on their political and civil rights, culture and socio-economic opportunities. A difference is that much of the contemporary discourse in the USA is around the question of apology and material reparation while in Australia these two factors are supplemented by the issue of the extent to which the national identity of indigenous Australians should be recognised, if at all, and whether this is in tension with a 'colour-blind' conception of citizenship.

Another significant difference between the two examples is that the apology in Australia seems to have gathered more support in recent years, based on the recorded reception to Rudd's apology, while in the USA it is not clear this is the case. Also, the extent of public discussion and debate and the degree of mobilisation around the issue seems greater in Australia. It is difficult to state definitively the reason; however the publication of the HREOC *Bringing Them Home* Report in 1997 would appear to be a factor here. It provoked and facilitated a public discussion which commentators have interpreted as opening a new chapter in the thinking about indigenous Australians and this may have contributed to the development of a more positive view concerning the apology. In the USA, in the period under discussion (approximately from the mid-1990s) there is no comparable event that informed or galvanised the debate about slavery or Jim Crow; positions were generally struck on the basis of already existing evidence and information.

The discussion here turns to the basis of support and opposition to the apology by Rudd in 2008. For comparison and points of reference, it is useful to record a summary of the findings of a study published in 2004 by Augoustinos and LeCouteur which analysed responses following Howard's 1997 address to the Reconciliation Convention. The four major rhetorical arguments used by those opposing the apology were: 'you have to be practical; present generations cannot be blamed for the mistakes of past generations; everybody should be treated equally; and resources should be used productively in a cost-effective manner'.[37] Three points will be highlighted about these constructions. First, the first and fourth arguments reflect Howard's focus on 'practical' reconciliation which seems particularly pertinent in the Australian debate and, as Burridge indicates above, is a construction favoured by conservatives. Second, the generational issue (argument two) reflects the question of responsibility which was identified in Chapter 3 as a significant aspect of potential critiques of the apology. Third, the equality of treatment argument reflects a liberal construction which is generally critical of group claims or policies favouring particular groups on the basis of past disadvantage. This echoes the point made in Chapter 4 that liberalism, generally speaking, is in tension with or hostile to the apology.

It is interesting to note, in light of the discussion above how the apology is understood and what it means, that the predominant position of supporters of the apology examined in this study was not feeling responsible or experiencing emotions such as blame or guilt; rather the apology was supported as an expression of sympathy or acknowledgement of past wrongs.[38] This indicates the variability of the impact of responsibility on positions; while those who accept the idea of responsibility across generations are likely to support apologies (in general though not necessarily in every instance), those who reject it may or may not support the apology.

Discourse

The following discussion is based upon the forum set up by the Australian Broadcasting Corporation (ABC) immediately after the Rudd apology in February 2008.[39] Many of the contributions and exchanges were vitriolic, intemperate and antagonistic, with reason and argument being of secondary concern. However, some insights into the way the apology was conceived of can be gleaned. At a general level, and bearing out the earlier hypothesis about the historical context and the 'insider' and 'outsider' construction, much of the discussion hinged on attitudes towards, and conceptualisations of indigenous Australians and reads like another playing-out of the 'history wars'. A series of assumptions and stereotypes were manifest: for example, all material and cultural progress could be attributed to white settlement, indigenous disadvantage could be wholly explained by fecklessness and that the indigenous population already benefited from disproportionate 'hand-outs' and public expenditure. Unsurprisingly, those holding such views opposed the apology. These views were often challenged from a more progressive perspective. What is striking about these exchanges is the radically different way in which

Australian history and the experience of the indigenous people is understood which largely renders a 'debate' useless since the positions are so far apart.

However, some more specific points about why the apology was opposed or supported can be deduced. In opposition, five themes recurred in the discussion.[40]

1 *Compensation*. In some contributions, it was felt that the apology would further either individual or collective claims for compensation. This had been done already through public expenditure: 'the Aboriginal people have been compensated in the form of millions of dollars of dedicated Aboriginal funding over many decades'. 'Compensation has been prepaid! If you care to look at the tremendous amount of money which has been targeted over many years and successive governments to one particular group of Australians then I think you will find that money is not the answer. Time to look forward! Same laws, rules and support for all Australians and no special cases.' This commentary reflects the position of those in the 2004 study of Augoustinos and LeCouteur who emphasised equal treatment and regarded the apology as an infringement of the principle.

2 *Responsibility*. 'I feel I have nothing to apologise for with regard to the stolen generation, because I had absolutely nothing to do with it.' 'Why should we be "sorry" I can understand feeling sympathy and that they were treated terribly but why should I have to be sorry I don't see the need to apologise for something most of us had absolutely nothing to do with.'(There was one counter to this position. One contributor stated: 'Australians cannot bask in inter-generational glory of the courage of my forbears at Gallipoli and Toobruk unless they are willing to accept the shame of our inter-generational wrongs – it is not a one way street.)'[41]

3 *Relationship between government and people*. This is related to point 2 but slightly different. Some argued the government could apologise because previous legislators were responsible but this could not extend to include all Australians: 'the error was theirs [lawmakers], not ours, so there is nothing for which today's generation of Australians need to feel remorse. Sympathy and regret, certainly, but not remorse, for that implies a responsibility which is not that of today's Australians.' The issue was also 'muddied' because it was not clear who was making the apology. As Augoustinos *et al.* have noted, there is some ambiguity in Rudd's use of 'we' which can be read as 'the nation' or 'the government'.[42] Some argued that an apology by the government did not include the people and one contributor seemed to argue that a government apology needed unanimous support among the people. 'Mr Rudd's position is to govern

for all Australians and I do not think he or any other Government has the right to apologise to anyone, without the "Consensus of all Australians".'

4 *Emotion* (which has overlap with point 3). Some theorists and commentators have argued that the political apology should be decoupled from the question of emotion; however many contributors made a link between the apology and an emotional engagement. Those who did not feel an emotional engagement, or felt ones which they did not relate to the concept of responsibility, as in the extract at point 3 above, were unlikely to support the apology. This relates to the point made in the introduction to this chapter about how the apology is understood. For example, if it seen principally as an acknowledgement of a past injustice then a particular emotional engagement is irrelevant; however many contributors to this site did associate the apology with an emotional stance that they did not share.

5 *Division*. Some of those who opposed the apology claimed that there was significant support for this position in Australia.[43] Their inference from this was the apology would create or cause further division in the country because the government did not speak for many of its citizens.

For those in favour of the apology, the two most cited reasons were:

1 *Acknowledgement*. 'I felt like a weight has lifted. It was necessary to acknowledge the truth – without hedging, without excuses, without explanations.' The term 'acknowledgement' was used in two different ways; one meaning relating to the truth of the 'Stolen Generation' and the other to the wider acknowledgement of the status as citizens and the value of the culture of indigenous Australians. As indicated in this quotation, many implicitly or explicitly contrasted Rudd's statement with the perceived inadequacies of those of Howard or Nelson.

2 *Reconciliation*. 'Finally, step one of the reconciliation process is done.' 'Now Australia can move on.' 'I feel that we have really turned a corner as a Nation and will move on together into a better future.'

The position regarding emotion of those favouring the apology was mixed; some interpreted the apology as either the recognition of a past wrong and/or a laudable attempt at reconciliation between white and indigenous Australians. This did not imply any personal guilt or shame although some contributors did articulate such emotions.

To conclude, attitudes to, and understanding of, indigenous peoples is the most salient factor in positions adopted. In relation to the issues discussed in Chapter 3, the question of responsibility and the associated debate is the most pertinent in the Australian case. The continuation of the child separation policy until the 1970s and the impact of the *Bringing Them Home* report meant that time, the feeling that 'it was a long time ago' was not an issue in the debate. The issue of the indeterminacy of the victims did not loom large, partly because for many opponents of the apology indigenous people were not victims but recipients of unwarranted privileged treatment.

The Bloody Sunday apology[44]

Chronology

The apology made for Bloody Sunday by British Prime Minister David Cameron in June 2010 came shortly after the publication of the Saville report by a commission which had been established in 1997 by Cameron's Labour predecessor, Tony Blair. Blair set up the Saville inquiry following evidence concerning the inadequacies of the original inquiry by Lord Widgery which was published in 1972. Although not part of a connected process as in the other two case studies discussed, the apology came after other actors in the Northern Ireland conflict had apologised in at least a qualified or circumscribed manner. This includes Blair's regret concerning British inaction at the time of the Potato Famine in the 1840s, issued in 1997. While not an apology directly connected to the Troubles, as noted in Chapter 1, it is best interpreted in the context of Anglo-Irish relations and the bilateral management of the complexities of the 'peace process'. In 1994, in the context of discussion over ceasefires, the Combined Loyalist Military Council, an umbrella group which represented the loyalist paramilitaries the Ulster Volunteer Force (UVF), the Ulster Defence Association (UDA) and the Red Hand Commandos (RHC) offered an apology to non-combatants killed in the Troubles and in 2002, the IRA offered a similar qualified apology.[45] Subsequently there have been apologies, or statements of regret, over killings of particular individuals including one by the British government in relation to security force collusion in the loyalist paramilitary killing of a solicitor, Pat Finucane and from the IRA for the killing of Garda (police officer of the Irish Republic) Jerry McCabe. The political context of the apology is indicated by the fact that the IRA continue to distinguish between the killing of Gardai members and members of the Northern Ireland police force (named the Royal Ulster Constabulary (RUC) in the period of the Troubles and later re-named the Police Service of Northern Ireland (PSNI) as part of the 'peace process' reforms).

Opinion poll

According to one opinion poll, the apology by Cameron was supported by 60 per cent of people in Britain and 70 per cent in Northern Ireland.[46] The poll did not break down respondents by community identity but the figures suggest that there was some support for the apology among the Unionist community. Historically, in Northern Ireland partisan allegiance and political attitudes were influenced, though not determined for all groups or individuals, by an ethno-national identification with either the unionist community (which wanted to retain political and cultural linkages with the UK) or the nationalist community (which wanted closer political and cultural ties with the Republic of Ireland). This is a schematic and over-simplified summary of the situation; however it does help to illuminate some of the positions struck in relation to the apology. Also, as with the two other case studies, there is a framing of 'insider' and 'outsider' with a perception among nationalists that they were an 'outsider' group; marginalised politically, economically and culturally within the Northern Ireland state. Fifteen years after the Good Friday Agreement of 1998 it is possible that these perceptions are changing, both within Northern Ireland itself and the British state; representatives of which have long stressed their support for the equal status of the two communities in Northern Ireland and endorsement of 'parity of esteem'.

Political context

Therefore, the political context of Cameron's apology was the years of conflict in Northern Ireland and the associated political divisions, and this provides a way to think about some of the responses. It is interesting that very few, if any, of the responses of political representatives in Northern Ireland denied that the shootings were an injustice or opposed the apology *in toto*. My argument is that the reasons for this are to do with the form of the injustice under consideration. Compared to the two case studies above, it is much more difficult to critique the Bloody Sunday apology within a framework of the concepts outlined in Chapter 3, in particular those of responsibility, time and indeterminacy. Even proponents of an apology for slavery and the treatment of indigenous Australians would not deny that there are many complexities and variables in assessing the impact of the phenomena involved. However, this does not seem to have the same pertinence in relation to Bloody Sunday. Cameron accepted British state responsibility. The *Guardian* blog report of the apology reported his position thus: ' Cameron has just said that he does not apologise lightly. He suggests that he disliked the way Tony Blair apologised for the Irish Famine. But he explained why he was apologising today. What happened on Bloody Sunday was wrong, the government of the day is no longer around, and so it fell to him to issue an apology instead.'[47] The issue of 'too long ago' was not relevant by any construction of time used; the events were recent and in living memory of anyone aged in their mid-forties or over in 2010. The indeterminacy of the victims of the injustice was likewise not an issue since those killed and wounded, the principal victims, were identifiable.

Discourse

Relatedly, the criticisms of the apology focused upon the political context, including the IRA campaign, the illegal nature of the march in Londonderry and the belief that the cost and duration of the Saville report was an indulgence of republican concerns. The interpretation that some Unionist representatives brought to bear on the outcome of the inquiry and the Cameron apology was that a hierarchy of victims had been created to the detriment of unionist victims. The following extracts provide a flavour of such thinking. Jeffrey Donaldson, the Democratic Unionist Party (DUP) MP, stated: 'the difficulty is that we have the truth on one side, but not the truth on the other. We don't know the truth about what Martin McGuinness and the IRA were doing on that day. While we regret every death … we must not lose sight of the need for balance.'[48] Leader of the Ulster Unionist Party (UUP), Sir Reg Empey stated: 'Clearly and rightly the onus will always be on ministers of the crown to account for the actions of the military, and today David Cameron shouldered that responsibility. However, while some families may have had a degree of closure today, very many others have not been so fortunate. In the days before Bloody Sunday, two RUC officers … were shot dead in the Creggan area of the city. Their families have not received justice.'[49] A particularly trenchant comment came from Jim Allister, leader of Traditional Unionist Voice (TUV) who said: 'My primary thoughts today are with the thousands of innocent victims of the IRA who have never had justice, nor benefitted from any inquiry into why their loved ones died. Thus, today's jamboree over the Saville report throws into very sharp relief the unacceptable and perverse hierarchy of victims which the preferential treatment of "Bloody Sunday" has created.'[50]

Responses among representatives thus fit fairly neatly along party lines and confessional or community identification, with the nationalist Social Democratic and Labour Party (SDLP) and the republican Sinn Fein statements containing no such qualifications. The politicised nature of the apology and the desire for unionists to gain some reciprocal recognition for the suffering of their community was indicated in September 2012, when the Northern Ireland Assembly approved a motion which called on the Irish government to apologise for its alleged role in the emergence of the IRA. The motion was tabled by the DUP and a UUP amendment made specific reference to the British apology for Bloody Sunday. Both Sinn Fein and SDLP opposed the motion, revealing again the partisan positions adopted in relation to the issue of apology.[51]

Conclusion

It is worth considering whether there are commonalities in the politics of the apology in these three intra-state examples. One way to think about them and the form they took is the articulation between the moral stance of the main protagonists and the political environment in which they operated. The former provides at least a partial explanation of why the apology occurred and the latter a partial explanation of why the apology took the form it did. Senator Harkin, who introduced the Senate resolution, Kevin Rudd and David Cameron all indicated that the apology was the morally correct thing to do. However, while principles and moral stances may inform these decisions, political considerations will influence or determine the form or extent of the apology. The Senate resolution which explicitly decoupled an apology from reparation and the lack of reparation to individuals connected to the Rudd apology were informed by the calculation that such provision would be politically unacceptable to many citizens. The 'other side of the coin' is that some of the recipients of the apology felt it to be inadequate though many did not.[52] However, there was little political cost for the governments emanating from such dissatisfaction since the numbers involved (perhaps a minority of a minority group within the polity) meant that they had limited political influence. The fact that apologies generally have low political salience also gives governments room for manoeuvre in their formulation.[53]

If the lack of reparation in the above two cases in seen by some as a lack of adequate 'follow-up ' (see Chapter 1), the comparison in the Bloody Sunday case study is that of the prosecution of soldiers responsible for the killings. To date, this has not occurred and it is possible such action would be considered by David Cameron as a politically unacceptable 'follow-up' and this judgement would be shared by much of the British electorate.

One similarity between the Australian and the Northern Ireland example which sets them apart from the American example is the significance of a specific and comprehensive report which frames the debate and the public engagement. As illustrated, this does not prevent criticism or rejection of the apology but does appear to influence the articulation of these critiques. Given the strong evidence base of the two reports and the contemporary nature of the events described, it was difficult to mount a critique based on the lack of veracity of the reports or the 'long time ago' argument outlined in Chapter 3. Such opposition as there was tended to reflect partisan sentiment related to the understanding of the political context and the conceptualisation of the 'other'.

Notes

1 R. Hague and M. Harrop, *Comparative Government and Politics* (Basingstoke: Palgrave Macmillan, 8th edn, 2010), pp. 161–77.
2 See Smith, *I Was Wrong* for the variety of forms of apologies.
3 These terms refer to the idea that, sociologically, people often adopt group identities and view negatively those outside the group. For a consideration of group identity and conflict between groups from a social psychology perspective, see the essays in L. R. Tropp (ed.), *The Oxford Handbook of Intergroup Conflict* (Oxford: Oxford University Press, 2012).
4 Nobles, *The Politics of Official Apologies*, pp. 104–7. The text of the resolution is in Brooks (ed.), *When Sorry Isn't Enough*, pp. 350–2.
5 *U.S. News and World Report*, 6 April 1998, p. 7 reproduced in *ibid.*, p. 352. The claim about reparation is found in Pettigrove, 'Apology, reparations and the question of inherited guilt', pp. 319–20, Brooks, 'Not even an Apology?', p. 312 and Coicaud, 'Apology', pp. 115–16.
6 Cited in K. D. Wenger, 'Apology lite: truths, doubts and reconciliations in the Senate's guarded apology for slavery', *CONNtemplations, Connecticut Law Review*, 42:1 (2009), 1–11, p. 10, n. 60.
7 E. B. Fleming, 'When Sorry Is Enough: the Possibility of a National Apology for Slavery', 95–108 in Gibney *et al.* (eds), *The Age of Apology*, p. 105.
8 Cited in Wenger, 'Apology lite', p. 2.
9 The 1997 poll is cited in J. R. Feagin and E. O' Brien, 'The Growing Movement for Reparations', 341–4 in Brooks (ed.), *When Sorry Isn't Enough*, p. 343. The 2000 poll is cited in M. Dawson and R. Popoff, 'Reparations: justice and greed in black and white', *Du Bois Review*, 1:1 (2004), 47–91, p. 61. The first 2002 poll is cited in 'Slavery-Reparations' http://law.jrank.org/pages/10314/slavery-REPARATIONS.html, accessed 11 March 2013, and the CNN/USA Today poll of 2002 is cited in W. Douglas, 'Congress apology for slavery just proves it's hard to say sorry', www.mcclatchydc.com/2009/07/02/71194/congress-apology-for-slavery-just.html, p. 3, accessed 8 March 2013. The 2008 poll is cited in R. Bilali and M. A. Ross, 'Remembering Intergroup Conflict', 123–35 in Tropp (ed.), *The Oxford Handbook of Intergroup Conflict* (Oxford: Oxford University Press, 2012), p. 129.
10 See Dawson and Popoff, 'Reparations'.
11 Extensive references can be found in Torpey, 'Paying for the past?' and M. Berg, 'Historical Continuity and Counterfactual History in the Debate over Reparations for Slavery', 69–91 in Berg and Schaefer (eds), *Historical Justice in International Perspective*.
12 For an example of the conservative position see D. Horowitz, *Uncivil Wars: The Controversy over Reparations for Slavery* (San Francisco: Encounter Books, 2002).
13 S. Con. Res. 26 cited in 'Senate Apology for Slavery Gets Mixed Reaction', www.npr.org/templates/story/story.php?storyId=105850676, p. 3, accessed 8 February 2013.
14 *Ibid.*
15 *Ibid.*
16 *Ibid.*
17 'The living consequences: exploring the legacy of slavery and race in the United States', http://living.jdewperry.com/209/06/senator-harkin-introduces-apology-for-slavery-and-racism,

accessed 8 February 2013. Subsequent quotations are from this document.

18 See, for example, the debate around slavery in British history in Cunningham, '"It wasn't us and we didn't benefit"'.

19 Celermajer, *The Sins of the Nation*, p. 154.

20 Thompson, 'Apology, Justice and Respect', pp. 40–1.

21 M. Augoustinos and A. LeCouteur, 'On Whether to Apologize to Indigenous Australians: the Denial of White Guilt', 236–61 in N. R. Branscombe and B. Doosje (eds), *Collective Guilt: International Perspectives* (Cambridge: Cambridge University Press, 2004), pp. 236–7.

22 B. Attwood, 'Settling Histories, Unsettling Pasts: Reconciliation and Historical Justice in a Settler Society', 217–38 in Berg and Schaefer (eds), *Historical Justice in International Perspective*, p. 232.

23 For example, see Augoustinos *et al.*, 'Apologizing for historical injustice'.

24 Augoustinos and Le Couteur, 'On Whether to Apologize to Indigenous Australians', p. 238.

25 Nobles, *The Politics of Official Apologies*, pp. 24, 97.

26 BBC News. 'Australia apology to Aborigines', 13 February 2008, http://news.bbc.co.uk/1/hi/7241965.stm, accessed 12 October 2012.

27 Weyeneth, 'The power of apology', p. 26, n. 54.

28 Celermajer, *The Sins of the Nation*, p. 178, n. 17.

29 Angus Reid, 'Australians back apologies for Stolen Generations', www.angus-reidglobal.com.polls/30819/australians-back-apology-for-stolen-generations, accessed 5 February 2013.

30 N. Burridge, 'Perspectives on reconciliation and indigenous rights', *Cosmopolitan Civil Societies Journal*, 1:2 (2009), 111–28, p. 126.

31 T. Smith, 'The letter, the spirit, and the future: Rudd's apology to Australia's Indigenous people', www.ausralianreview.net/digest/2008/03/smith.html, p. 3, accessed 12 October 2012.

32 Nobles, *The Politics of Official Apologies*, pp. 98–9.

33 The African-American proportion of the population of the USA was approximately 13.1 per cent in 2011. US Department of Commerce, United States Census Bureau, www.quickfacts.census.gov/qfd.states.00000.html, accessed 13 March 2013. The indigenous population of Australia was estimated at 2.6 per cent of the total population in 2011. Australian Bureau of Statistics cited in Australian Indigenous HealthInfoNet, www.healthinfonet.ecu.edu/au/health-facts/aboriginal-population, accessed 13 March 2013.

34 For a diagrammatic representation and more detail, see Burridge, 'Perspectives on reconciliation and indigenous rights', p. 116.

35 *Ibid.*, pp. 116–17.

36 Burridge claims this is the most popular with 'mainstream Australians', *ibid.*, p. 116.

37 Augoustinos and LeCouteur, 'On Whether to Apologize to Indigenous Australians', p. 253.

38 *Ibid.*, p. 247.

39 Australian Broadcasting Corporation, 'What do you think about saying "Sorry?"', www.abc.net.au/unleashed/37092.html, accessed 8 February 2013.

40 The following extracts quoted are from the website (*ibid.*); grammar and spelling are as in original. There is no pagination in the text used.

41 Celermajer makes a similar point in *The Sins of the Nation*, p. 184.

42 Augoustinos *et al.*, 'Apologizing for historical injustice', p. 515.

43 However most opinion polls suggest otherwise.

44 See also discussion in Chapter 2.

45 For more details of the apologies of Blair and the IRA, see Cunningham, 'Apologies in Irish Politics'.

46 Angus Reid, 'Britons and Northern Irish welcome PMs Apology for Bloody Sunday'.

47 A. Sparrow, 'Politics live with Andrew Sparrow. Bloody Sunday: the Saville report as it happened', www.guardian.co.uk/news/blog/2012/jun/15bloodysunday-northernireland, p. 27, accessed 1 February 2013.

48 BBC News Northern Ireland, 'Bloody Sunday report published', 15 June 2010, www.bbc.co.uk/news/10322708, p. 2, accessed 1 February 2013.

49 *Ibid.*, p. 2.

50 *Ibid.*, p. 3.

51 BBC News Northern Ireland, 'Assembly motion calls for Irish government apology,' 18 September 2012. www.bbc.co.uk/news/uk-northernireland-19631027, accessed 7 December 2012.

52 It is difficult to quantify, although the majority of the indigenous people of Australia were supportive of the Rudd apology. Wenger records a mixed response to the Senate apology but indicates qualified support among many African-Americans (Wenger, 'Apology lite').

53 Nobles makes this point in relation to Australia; however her book was written before the Rudd apology of 2008 (Nobles, *The Politics of Official Apologies*, p. 24).

6

Inter-state apologies and International Relations

It was stated in the introduction that the study of the apology had been informed and influenced by several disciplines; however international relations (IR) as a discipline has been slow in addressing the phenomenon of the apology. The vast majority of IR textbooks have no index entries for the apology and the majority of case studies of inter-state apologies do not draw explicitly on IR theory.[1] The purpose of this chapter is to address two broad issues; why states apologise to other states and whether these apologies are successful.

Given the claim above of the lack of 'link up' between the apology literature and the IR literature, the opening section will try to locate thinking about the inter-state apology within some of the traditions of IR for elucidation. One of the dominant traditions within IR is that of realism. To summarise, this tradition emphasises the role of power, security and the pursuit of self-interest in explanation of state activity on the international stage. It is assumed that self-interest is universal and a constant in explaining what states do, based on a rational calculation of costs and benefits.

These realist assumptions in IR have been challenged by the school of constructivism. While constructivism does not deny that self-interest can or does impel a nation's foreign policy and international interactions, it is critical of realism for not focusing sufficiently on how the interests of a nation or state are constructed; for example the importance of context, international norms and a state's identity in influencing state behaviour. In this way, the constructivist critique of realism in IR can be seen as comparable to sociological and communitarian critiques of rational choice theories and constructions of *homo economicus* which argue that the idea of 'interest' must be situated and developed against a backdrop of social and normative influences. To put it another way, according to Reus-Smit, two of constructivism's core ontological propositions concern the importance of normative or ideational structures in shaping the behaviour of social or political actors and the role of identities in informing interests and actions.[2] Arguably the phenomenon of the apology fits well within such an analysis because of the emphasis on the normative and the construction (and reconstruction) of identity and the emphasis on the variability of political practice within the constructivist tradition.

It is fruitful to consider the inter-state apology through the prism of two concepts. One can be termed *state interest*. This covers the range of benefits that can accrue to a state through diplomacy and other inter-state interactions that the realist tradition has focused upon, such as security, power and economic advantage. The second can be termed *state identity* and reflects the insights that constructivism offers. The idea of state identity has two aspects. One is that states have ways of 'seeing themselves' which are informed by a political culture that may change over time. This idea draws on the work of Katzenstein who argues, contrary to realists, that culture and identity have an independent explanatory power and that states are social actors and their political identities need to be studied in specific historical contexts.[3] The second aspect is that states have a conception of international norms and standards that may influence their activities and policies in relation to the identity they are trying to project. Both of these elements together suggest that the action of states (or of certain states at certain times) cannot be reduced to, or explained by, the concept of state interest which social constructivists believe realists see as unproblematic. It may be objected that a good image or identity of a state is in its interest so a realist account can satisfactorily subsume the idea of state identity. However, in theory and empirically states can and do apologise in contexts where self-interest is absent or not a primary concern in a way that realism articulates it.[4]

There are two other features of the political apology that need to be borne in mind in trying to think about the apology in relation to inter-state relations. These may not hold for every apology made, since the contingent and specific elements of the apology have been stressed throughout this book. However, many apologies will introduce a specifically normative element into the process of inter-state relations given that apologies, even qualified and attenuated ones, imply some degree of responsibility for the committing of an injustice or injustices. Second, the state apology is, in practice, bound up with an implicit or explicit critique of the history of the state or nation. This is significant because one aspect of the state's foreign policy (the apology) becomes closely linked with what is often a matter of more widespread communal and domestic concern; the representation of the nation's history. The representation of a nation's history is often a politically contentious topic as was noted in Chapter 5 and is also considered further in Chapter 7.

The implication of these two points is that the apology tends to undermine and work against a *realpolitik* conception of international relations in which normative issues are downplayed and against some of the practices of diplomacy and inter-state relations which located them within the sphere of high politics. In this sphere, the practices of policy-makers operated in relative isolation from domestic pressures and perceptions. This is not to claim that historically the foreign policy of particular nations could not have an ethical dimension or engage the emotions of the populace; rather that the apology seems to imply a need to account for and reckon with these factors.[5]

The following sections will attempt to map the ideas of state interest and state identity against one explanation of state apology and then try to illustrate some of the reasons for the apology and the question of success or failure through some concrete examples.

As argued in the introduction to this chapter, there has been relatively little work explicitly about IR and state apologies. However, Bilder recently offered a list of reasons why states do (and do not) apologise.[6] He outlined seven reasons why states apologise: they genuinely believe it to be the right thing to do; because of the binding judgment of an international court; because an apology will contribute to establishing or reinforcing some 'desired customary law rule or treaty interpretation'; it is a low-cost way of resolving or defusing an incident; to 'get away' with a bad act; because they are being coerced into it; or as a cynical PR gesture for the international community. The first and third of these reasons would seem to fit with an idea of normative standards of state action or normative standards within the international community that the idea of a state identity alluded to above, while four of the other five reasons can be explained within a realist framework which would emphasise the 'rational' assessment of the costs and benefits of the apology.

The remaining reason is that of coercion. This is worthy of a little more discussion for two reasons. First, it could be argued that the coercion of a state into an apology falls outside the two organising concepts of state interest and state identity. If the sole reason for a state apology is coercion by another it neither represents a reasoned cost– benefit analysis associated with interest nor does it exhibit a degree of reflection or assessment of normative values associated with state identity. This position is given some credence in that it reflects Wendt's tripartite explanation of state action: coercion, self-interest and legitimacy, with the later two paralleling the concepts of interest and identity used here.[7] Second, it is debatable how coercion might be defined or conceptualised as a factor in a state apology. The use of force or the threat of force by another party would seem to be clear examples. However it is possible to conceive of pressure put upon a state with weak bargaining power in the international arena because of, for example, social disintegration or economic crisis, as a form of coercion.[8]

Conversely, Bilder offers five reasons why states do not apologise. They do not believe they have done wrong; the apology could open the way for litigation as the apology implies responsibility; the apology may lend support to customary rule or treaty interpretation that the state opposes; the apology is seen as demeaning or will attract domestic criticism; or that there is no political need as no disadvantage will accrue from not apologising. Similarly, the first and fourth explanations could be usefully examined through the prism of state identity, and how the state sees itself and understands the norms of the international community, while the other three fit within a realist account of costs and benefits.

To explore some of these themes further, particular examples of state apologies will be examined. This will not allow the claim to be made that all reasons for the inter-state apology have been adduced or that it can be definitively judged whether apologies are successful. This would require more detailed case studies. However, by looking at a sample of apologies in different contexts some insights will be gleaned into the issues raised and the applicability of the concepts used above.

The five examples to be considered are the apologies of Japan to China and particularly Korea; those of Germany to various states for the Second World War; the reciprocal apologies of states emerging from the break-up of the former Yugoslavia; Clinton's apology to Rwanda and Guatemala; and Blair's apology to the Irish Republic in relation to the famine. The considerations of each will have three parts, some of the salient detail, the reasons the apologies were offered and the question of success.

Any consideration of the literature on Japanese apologies quickly reveals two features. First, is the sheer number of apologies that has been issued. One estimate made in 2005 was that Japan had issued thirty-six 'official' apologies since 1973 for its conduct in the Second World War and the total number of Japanese apologies by 2012, including to non-state actors, probably exceeds fifty.[9] There is some irony here given that Japan is often perceived as a nation which has not apologised. The second feature is despite, or because of, the number of apologies how contentious they have been. There are two elements here that should be highlighted but will not be explored in depth. The series of Japanese apologies has been accompanied by a domestic 'backlash'. In fact, according to Lind, the relationship is closer than this. She states 'in Japanese politics, apologies and denials do not simply coexist: apologies (or proposed apologies) frequently *cause* denials'.[10] A feature of Japanese apologies has been the replaying of their perceived inadequacies by recipients and conservative forces domestically denouncing their being offered. The second element is that there has been much discussion, both by recipients and commentators, concerning the linguistic adequacy of the apology. As noted in Chapter 1, there is much debate about the linguistic component of the apology and the necessity or not of the IFID.

This seems particularly pertinent in the case of Japan which relates to two factors: the use of partial and attenuated forms of apology by leaders in the context of domestic opposition and the nuances of the Japanese language which has led to heated exchanges concerning which term, word or phrase should be used to express a thorough-going apology.[11] These problems with Japanese apologies relate to what, in a different context, Renner has called the 'perlocutionary' effects.[12] This refers to the unintended and often negative effects and impacts apologies can have. This is particularly a problem in inter-state apologies where there are frequently, if not always, three parties interpreting, and responding to, the apology; the domestic audience, the recipient audience and the international audience. Therefore, what the apology 'means' is open to interpretation and its intended effects can 'escape' from those who offer it.

How are the motivations behind the Japanese apologies to be assessed? It would be counter-intuitive to expect that Japan had offered apologies to other states without some conception of state interest. This motivation as an explanation can be found in four texts that deal in some detail with Japanese apologies.[13] The chapter title concerning Japan in Negash's text is 'A Political Calculus of Apology' which has clear overtones of a realist approach to political action. He concludes by arguing that: 'the political calculus of apology between Japan and its neighbours, other than reconciliation, is more discernable as they have more to do with normalization and power politics'.[14] This sentence is a little unclear as 'normalization' is not defined or explained at length but it is clear that Negash argues that a factor in the explanation of Japanese apologies is that of a calculation of state interest in relation to areas including increased trading links with China and the pursuit of a seat at the UN Security Council to allow Japan to play a global peacekeeping role.[15] A similar discussion of Japanese interest can be found in Dudden. She claims that the extent to which states participated in apology politics, which date from the mid-1980s, depended on local aspirations to power in the international system. From the early 1990s in Japan 'official apologies became deeply entwined with the pursuit of national interests, and the country's conservative party, in particular, veered towards the practice. Leaders maintained that it was pragmatic for Japan to apologise for something called "the past" because doing so would affirm the nation's current and future ties with its Asian neighbors.'[16]

Yamazaki's study of the apology in Japan differs from the others in that it is a study of the rhetoric of apology; however, as in the other accounts, a clear perception of state interest is a factor in the apology or in specific apologies. One example is the apology of Prime Minister Hosokawa of November 1993. In a visit to South Korea he made an apology which was based upon 'the immediate needs of cooperation in strategic and economic issues'.[17]

State interest is clearly a factor at play here. However, another central theme in the texts is the way in which the apology, or apologies, relate to Japan's position within the international community. While the concept of 'international community' is not always clearly defined, certain inferences may be drawn from its use. In the sentence cited above, Negash seems to be distinguishing between reconciliation and power politics/interests as motivations or reasons for apology. It may be inferred from this that there are reasons for the apology that go beyond a narrow conceptualisation of state interest and are connected to a state's desire to have better relations with former adversaries. A counter to this point may be that such reconciliation may bring rewards or benefits that chime with a construction of state interest; however Negash can be read as suggesting these are different motivations.

The work of Dudden has a similar focus in that alongside the state interests just outlined is the argument that the apology helps to 'define those issuing them as "normal" or "good-standing" members of the global community'.[18] In the conclusion of her book, she claims that 'saying sorry for certain histories gained traction once those making the apologies discovered in them a means with which to reinstate the nation in the international system'.[19] Neither 'global community' nor 'international system' is defined further in the text so it is not clear if they are synonyms or have a precise meaning. However, one reading of this text is that Japan has apologised because of its desire to be integrated, or possibly reintegrated, into an international community that has shared normative values.

Yamazaki argues that the state apology in general can and does have multiple motivations including political advantage (compatible with state interest above), the repair of relationship and the affirmation of moral principle. In Japan's case, Yamazaki emphasises that the apology is set against a background of notions of both self-identity and a conception of international norms. For example, the apology of Hosokawa in 1993 is interpreted as a 'break with the past' in which 'by acknowledging past wrongdoing, the body politic purges its guilt and can start afresh with a new sense of identity and self-worth'.[20] This allows Japan to present itself as a 'peace nation' and pave its way for integration into the international community. In similar vein, in 1995 on the occasion of the fiftieth anniversary of the end of the Second World War, part of the speech of the socialist Prime Minister Murayama emphasised that Japan had a new mission which was 'to be a good member of the world community'.[21] The point to be emphasised here is that these uses of the apology are only comprehensible if Japan (or some of its political leaders) have a conception that there are international norms which a state can attempt to meet whether through a changing of its ways or by a distancing from its past self.[22]

In her conclusion Yamazaki argues that there are three motivations for Japan's apologies. The first is the repairing of relationships, the second is the construction of a new moral identity and the third is the 'affirmation of moral principle'. The third is the most interesting in relation to the question of the international community. Yamazaki writes: 'Apology is the price for readmission into society's good graces, the price for restoring legitimacy. Thus, the transcendent apology for moral principle is more or less coerced and can be seen as a ritual of submission to outside or societal authority.'[23] How is this to be interpreted? The transcendent apology is one which is not specific to a wronged group or the wronged group may be dead so it transcends the specific or concrete. 'Outside authority' here can be read as international society and the notion of coercion suggests that the distancing of the state from its former transgressing self is done for pragmatic rather than moral reasons; although the earlier sections seem to suggest that Murayama did have a sincere desire to critique Japan's past actions from a normative perspective. However, even if the apology is coerced this does not alter the fact that fully to understand the apology in Japan, or Japanese apologies, the idea of a world community which is constituted by normative values has to be part of the picture.

To summarise, the argument is that to capture fully the processes and forms of Japanese apologies one has to think about them in relation to state interests, but also to focus upon the identity of the Japanese state; how it sees itself and how others see it. These latter factors are here labelled 'state identity'.

The third issue to be addressed was whether Japanese apologies had been successful. This is difficult to say definitely because of the overlapping motivations and the sheer number of apologies to assess. However, it is clear that the objective of better relations with close neighbours and the construction of a better image for their consumption has not been realised since it was reported in autumn 2012 that visits by Japanese politicians to the shrine of war-heroes and a tougher stance on apologies by the new leader of the Liberal Democratic party had strained relations with Korea and China.[24] The common perception that Japan is a country that does not apologise, or does not apologise well, may indicate that the international perception of Japan is still negative, although this is harder to gauge.

A review of the position of Germany in relation to the Second World War can act as comparison.[25] As above, this will have three parts in which some of the salient points will be highlighted and a discussion of motivations and an evaluation of success will be offered. The first apology was made in 1951 by Chancellor Adenauer of the FDR to Israel.[26] The next was the famous 'knee-fall' by Chancellor Brandt at the site of the Warsaw ghetto in 1970. In the more contemporary 'age of apology' there have been apologies by President Weizsacker in 1985 on the fortieth anniversary of Germany's wartime defeat, by President Herzog to Poland in 1994, a joint and reciprocal apology to the Czech Republic in 1997, one by President Rau to Israel in 2000, one by

Chancellor Schroeder to Russia in 2005 and another to Israel by Chancellor Merkel in 2006.

The separate apologies will not be examined in detail; rather some general observations will be made about them. First, there appears to be a consensus among commentators that, over time, Germany's acceptance of war shame and guilt, and the willingness to mark it, has become more pronounced and is reflected in less qualified language. As Löwenheim records, there was a large degree of *realpolitik* in Adenauer's statement.[27] By contrast, Brandt's 'kneefall', a silent act of contrition with no accompanying words, is frequently cited in the literature on apology and held up as an exemplar of an act of repentance and expression of guilt. For example, Gibney and Roxstrom describe it as 'perhaps the most noteworthy, and certainly the most memorable, state apology' and, according to Celermajer, it was seen as helping to influence Eastern European politics as well as German–Polish relations.[28] Coicaud notes that for many (though he does not specify them) Weizsacker's apology of 1985 was even more effective than Brandt's and that Merkel's apology of 2006 seemed to indicate 'that a gradual process of internalization of responsibility for the past has been taking place in Germany'.[29] In respect of Rau's statement to the Knesset in 2000, Celermajer notes that: 'In just a little under fifty years, the language had shifted from gingerly linking Germany and the Holocaust via the name of the German people to identifying the German people as themselves responsible for the Holocaust and locating them in the aspect of repentance'.[30]

Similarly, Lind has periodised the development of attitudes and responses to the Second World War and the Holocaust. The West German exploration of its Nazi past began during the 'social-liberal era' of the 1960s and 1970s. A conservative 'backlash' of the 1980s was contained and by the late 1980s there was a bipartisan commitment to remembrance that transcended party lines. By the 1990s, which Lind terms the 'late period', there was much recognition of, and contrition about, the past reflected in speeches, museums, memorials and exhibitions.[31]

This links to the second point to be made here. By comparison with Japan, the 'backlash' from the German people towards these trends is muted. The far right has periodically resisted these trends but, as Lind points out, it has been contained. Both the political elite and the majority of German people have acknowledged wartime responsibility and guilt to an extent that appears absent in Japan. Given the attitudinal nature of some indicators, it is hard to measure precisely; however this seems to be a reasonable inference based on the available sources.

The above discussion would suggest that Germany's motivation for apology has changed over time from one of state interest to one where the concept of state identity is useful to explain the succession of apologies. The geo-political situation at the time of Adenauer's apology would seem to be an imperative in Germany making some acknowledgement of its wartime role. However, in the period of increasing apologies from the mid-1980s it is less clear that Germany needed to make these apologies; 'needed' in the sense that it had specific, instrumental gains to be achieved. Since approximately the late 1950s the geo-politics of the Cold War, West Germany's leading role in the foundation of the European Economic Community (EEC) and its economic recovery and strength would indicate that West Germany (and later the reunited Germany) was both a state whose strength indicated it could not be easily coerced and one whose functional integration into European alliances and relationship with the USA indicated its changed status and democratic commitments.

The point to be emphasised here is that while state interests may not be absent from the equation, the flurry of wartime-related apologies is better explained as an ongoing project to recast the state identity for the consumption of neighbours and the international community. Also, Germany is one of those cases whereby the apologies are made for the benefit of the apologiser as well in that Germany is trying to 'distance' itself from the Nazi manifestation of the German state. As Lind has noted, reconciliation between France and Germany preceded the age of apology which indicates that apology is not required, or not in all cases, for processes of inter-state reconciliation.[32]

In relation to the question of success, the reception of German apologies (allied to the payment of reparations or compensation) indicates that apologies may have played a role in reinforcing Germany's standing within the international community as the break with (and yet connection to) the Nazi past is emphasised. What is less clear is that such apologies were necessary given the apologies made in the preceding era and Germany's strategic and economic power within the post-war European order.

The third example to be considered is that of the former Yugoslavia. The violent break-up of the Yugoslavian state in the mid-1990s is a classic study in the conditions likely to produce a 'backlash' in the event of apologies. Strong nationalist sentiments fuelled by the conflict and drawing on Second World War memories and grievances were held by many of the protagonists. This meant that they opposed an apology either because they believed their community or nation to be the wronged party or because an apology was perceived as weakness. At best for some, an apology should only be offered reciprocally as the conditions of war meant that every side could point to injustices or atrocities committed by the other.

The 'backlash' is one of the key phenomenona in understanding the apologies issued by Serbia and Croatia; the other is the political aspiration of European Union (EU) accession shared by the Balkan states. These factors were in tension as the 'backlash' was a high domestic cost for the states involved whereas the perceived advantage of EU membership underpinned by the apology was a domestic benefit.[33]

Thus, the apologies of 2004 to 2007 were marked by ambiguity in an attempt to balance these conflicting objectives, and apologies tended to be marked by the linguistic evasions and qualifications which have been highlighted here, including holding particular citizens responsible for crimes and injustices rather than conceding state guilt or responsibility. While there was opposition to these attenuated apologies, the formulations helped to contain it. However, in 2010, the Serbian parliament passed a resolution acknowledging the massacre of Srebrenica in 1995 as a condition of its submission for EU membership of December 2009. According to Denti, the phase of apologies reached a watershed in November 2010 when Serbian and Croatian leaders made a joint visit to Vukovar which seemed to satisfy victims' demands for the admission of transgressions and reassurances concerning future conduct.[34]

This short summary of the Balkan apologies is useful to highlight three particular themes. First, the significance and resonance of the 'backlash' that is also important in the study of Japan. Second, the way in which a specific political objective, in this case the common goal of EU accession, can shape the apology process. Third, the extent to which the international community as 'audience' for the apology is important and perhaps to a greater degree than the nominal recipient of the apology.

The penultimate example is that of two of Clinton's apologies in the area of foreign policy. In March 1998 Clinton delivered a statement at Kigali airport in Rwanda expressing regret for his failure, but also that of 'the international community, together with nations, in Africa' to do more to prevent the Rwandan genocide of 1994. In March 1999, while on a tour of Central America, he made a statement in Guatemala concerning US support for right-wing regimes which had committed numerous human rights abuses over the previous thirty years. One reporting of this statement read: 'it is important that I state clearly that support for military forces and intelligence units which engaged in violence and widespread repression was wrong, and the US must not repeat that mistake'.[35]

The apologies of Clinton fell short of 'ideal type' apologies discussed in Chapter 1 in many ways and attracted much criticism.[36] Some of these shortcomings will be considered before attempting to explain why these (qualified) apologies were made. First, the language used was full of qualifications, evasions and there was a degree of disingenuousness about the statements. No IFIDs were involved in either, and in the Kigali speech Clinton spoke on behalf of others for which he had no mandate. He also implied that it was ignorance of the situation that prevented US involvement in Rwanda rather than a decision based on the political costs and benefits of intervention. Similarly, the rendering of US support for repressive regimes in Central and Latin America as a 'mistake' fails to emphasise the consistency of a policy informed by geo-political considerations in the context of the Cold War and a defence of US economic interests and investment.

Second, the 'performative' aspect was lacking in that the Kigali speech was held in an informal setting and there was little attempt to engage domestic interest or publicity for the speeches. In Gibney and Roxstrom's analysis, this is another way in which the apologies fell short of what they consider desired criteria for state apologies.[37] They argue that is it unclear why Clinton failed to engage the American people. Two possible reasons are that the policies were not of sufficient importance to warrant the deployment of resources of time and money to publicise further, or a calculation that many or most Americans would not endorse the apology and, low-key as it was, it was subject to some Republican criticism.[38]

This brings us to an attempt to explain why Clinton made these apologies, or, if one prefers, quasi-apologies. It is difficult to identify a clear state interest that fits easily with a realist construction of foreign policy determinants. Such is the power and international significance of the USA, and the relative insignificance of Guatemala and Rwanda, it is difficult to see any particular benefit that accrued to the USA, for example, in terms of security, regional hegemony or economic advantage. An alternative view is that the post-Cold War conjuncture allowed Clinton, the first president of this era, to signal the potential for a different kind of foreign policy. This could include the idea of a state identity formed around the notion of a commitment to intervene that reflects the purchase of international human rights and the wrongness of supporting dictatorial or condoning human rights abuses for reasons of *realpolitik*.

The concept of state identity reflects the potential importance of values and Smith indicates that Clinton issued what Smith terms 'the Value-Declaring Apology'. This type of apology 'primarily serves to announce the values of the speaker (or denounce the acts of others) and to commit her to honoring those principles. The apologizer does not accept personal blame for the past wrongdoing but instead proclaims that actions committed by others were wrong and vows not to commit similar offenses.'[39] As with other examples outlined above, this form of apology captures the attempt to differentiate the current actions, or potential trajectory, of the state from its past wrongdoing.

The final example is Tony Blair's statement about the Irish Famine made in 1997, which contains some clear parallels with the Clinton apologies. First, there was the lack of an explicit IFID with no use of the word 'sorry' or 'apologise'. Second, the 'performative' aspect of the apology was under-developed as the apology was delivered by an intermediary at a relatively 'low key' event. Third, there was little attempt to engage the British public and the domestic audience with a view to a wider popular endorsement.

As discussed above in Chapter 1, this apology can be viewed as part of a longer process of diplomatic interactions and initiatives with the Republic of

Ireland in an attempt to manage bilaterally 'the Troubles' in Northern Ireland. In this way, the apology can be seen as compatible with a state interest of security and conflict management found in realist theory. What is less clear is the necessity or the imperative of the apology given that close bilateral ties had existed since at least the early 1980s and had been strengthened by the Anglo-Irish Agreement of 1985. It can perhaps be viewed as a small part of a much wider and more complex network of initiatives to cement inter-state relations.

There are also overtones or echoes of state identity here in that the famine apology can be seen as an attempt to claim that the contemporary British state is a better one that its predecessor in that it has a greater sense of political and moral responsibility. The reference made to the failings of the earlier British administration can be interpreted as an attempt to fashion a state identity of responsibility and compassion to be contrasted with the former self.[40]

In conclusion, these five examples have illustrated the diversity of forms and contexts of the apology in inter-state relations. Whether an apology is made and the form it takes will be influenced by a number of factors including the ideology of particular leaders, an assessment of domestic costs and benefits, a perception of the likely reception by the recipient (which itself depends on the existant relationship), the likely reception by the international community which is influenced by evaluation of normative rules and principles that inform inter-state relations and the relative power of the state in the global order.

Two other points should be highlighted. First, although state interests inform the apology, a full understanding of the emergence and dynamics of state apologies needs to consider the image and identity a state tries to project, how that is constructed and how that articulates with normative values in the international order. This is where a constructivist theory of international relations offers more reward than a realist perspective. Second, it seems that the contribution of the apology to reconciliation is relatively modest. In none of these cases did the apology seem to be crucial in the process of reconciliation (or the lack of it). Although generalisations are dangerous given the emphasis above on the variety of apologies, a more common objective of the apology is to try to distance the state from its former 'bad' self which may offer some reassurance to the recipient of the apology. It needs to be borne in mind that reconciliation between states may commonly need less 'deep' forms than within states where after, for example, civil wars or authoritarian regimes, previously antagonistic groups have to live in the same reconstructed polities and previously oppressed groups have to live with their former oppressors.

Notes

1 Exceptions include N. Löwenheim, 'A haunted past: requesting forgiveness for wrongdoing in International Relations', *Review of International Studies*, 35:3 (2009), 531–55; J. Renner, '"I'm sorry for apologising": Czech and German apologies and their perlocutionary effects', *Review of International Studies*, 37:4 (2011), 1579–97; S. Jones, 'Apology diplomacy: justice for all?', Discussion Papers in Diplomacy, Netherlands Institute of International Relations, 'Clingendael', 2011, and D. Denti, 'Public apologies in the Western Balkans: the shadow of ambiguity', paper presented at 'The Ritual of Public Apology' workshop, UCSIA, Antwerp, March 2012, revised version August 2012.

2 C. Reus-Smit, 'Constructivism', 212–36 in S. Burchill, A. Linklater, R. Devetak, J. Donnelly, T. Nardin, M. Paterson, C. Reus-Smit and J. True, *Theories of International Relations* (Basingstoke: Palgrave Macmillan, 4th edn, 2009), pp. 220–1. For a review of constructivist ideas, see J. T. Checkel, 'The constructivist turn in International Relations theory', *World Politics*, 50: 2 (1998), 324–48.

3 R. Katzenstein, 'Introduction: Alternative Perspectives on National Security', 1–32 in R. Katzenstein (ed.), *The Culture of National Security: Norms and Identity in World Politics* (New York: Columbia University Press, 1996).

4 Examples will be developed later in this chapter.

5 Again, it seems to me constructivism can capture this better than realist conceptions of state action.

6 Bilder, 'The Role of Apology in International Law'.

7 Löwenheim, 'A haunted past', p. 533.

8 For example, the question of whether it could be claimed that Greece has been 'coerced' into acceptance of the EU austerity package.

9 The first figure is from Renner, '"I'm sorry for apologising"', p. 1583 and the second is author estimate based on various sources.

10 Lind, *Sorry States*, p. 94, emphasis in original.

11 See Yamazaki, *Japanese Apologies for World War II*. This is discussed in relation to British POWs in M. Cunningham, 'Prisoners of the Japanese and the politics of apology: a battle over history and memory', *Journal of Contemporary History*, 39:4 (2004), 561–74.

12 Renner, '"I'm sorry for apologising"'.

13 Negash, *Apologia Politica*; A. Dudden, *Troubled Apologies Among Japan, Korea and the United States* (New York: Columbia University Press, 2008); Lind, *Sorry States*; Yamazaki, *Japanese Apologies for World War II*.

14 Negash, *Apologia Politica*, p. 70.

15 *Ibid.*, p. 71.

16 Dudden, *Troubled Apologies*, p. 33.

17 Yamazaki, *Japanese Apologies for World War II*, p. 86.

18 Dudden, *Troubled Apologies*, p. 33.

19 *Ibid.*, p. 131.

20 Yamazaki, *Japanese Apologies for World War II*, p. 77.

21 *Ibid.*, p. 105.

22 Yamazaki likens this to the individual apology in trying to distance oneself from one's past self.

23 *Ibid.*, p. 128.
24 M. Dickie, 'Former Japan PM to lead opposition', *Financial Times* (27 September 2012), p. 10; J. McCurry, 'Outrage as MPs visit "shrine of war criminals"', *Guardian* (19 October 2012), p. 38.
25 For a comparative study of the way the two countries remember the war see I. Buruma, *The Wages of Guilt: Memories of War in Germany and Japan* (London: Phoenix, 2002).
26 See Löwenheim, 'A haunted past' for details.
27 *Ibid.*
28 Gibney and Roxstrom, 'The status of state apologies', p. 928. Celermajer, *The Sins of the Nation*, pp. 17–18.
29 Coicaud, 'Apology', p. 98.
30 Celermajer, *The Sins of the Nation*, pp. 18–19.
31 Lind, *Sorry States*, pp. 127–49.
32 *Ibid.*, p. 3.
33 This analysis draws heavily on Denti, 'Public apologies in the Western Balkans'.
34 *Ibid.*, pp. 9–10.
35 *New York Times* (11 March 1999), p. A12, cited in M. Cunningham, 'Mea Culpa (almost): Clinton, atrocity and the politics of apology', unpublished paper, 2005, p. 4.
36 One of the characters in Rayner's *The Apologist* compares the inadequacy of this apology with the exemplar of Brandt's 'kneefall'. See also n. 28 above.
37 Gibney and Roxstrom, 'The status of state apologies'.
38 As noted before, many Republicans view the apology as weakness. Mitt Romney's autobiographical manifesto for the 2012 US presidential campaign was entitled *No Apology: The Case for American Greatness* (New York: St Martin's Press, 2010). During the third presidential candidate debate in October 2012, Romney accused President Obama of having been on an apology tour of the Middle East. In 1979, the Republican presidential candidate of 1964, Barry Goldwater published a book entitled *With No Apologies: The Opinionated Political Memoirs of American Conservatism's Conscience* (New York: William Morrow, 1979). See also Smith, *I Was Wrong*, p. 193.
39 Smith, *I Was Wrong*, p. 148.
40 The text of Blair's statement is cited in Chapter 1.

7

Evaluating the apology: advantages and disadvantages

It was noted in earlier chapters that the majority of writers on the apology adopt a broadly positive view towards the phenomenon and emphasise its potential for bringing about benefits and gains to both the victims of injustice and those responsible for causing the injustice. This chapter will begin with a consideration of these potential benefits and then discuss the counter arguments deployed against the apology. The subsequent two sections will consider areas which are underdeveloped in the existing literature; the extent to which the apology actually delivers good outcomes and the relationship between the state and demos concerning the apology.

The (potential) benefits of the apology: why it is, or can be, good

The following section is based on a representative sample of material on the apology and will cite authors in support of particular positions. It should be noted that the potential benefits might not apply to all apologies; as indicated in previous chapters context and specificity is often important. The classification of the potential benefits of the apology is fourfold: those aspects that benefit the victims of injustice, those that benefit the victims and the apologiser (or those assuming responsibility for redress), those that benefit the apologiser and those which extend beyond the parties directly involved. There may be some degree of overlap in such classification and some of the terms may be open to contestation; however it is a useful way to analyse the claims.

There are three main benefits to the victims of the injustice contained in the apology. The first can be termed 'the recording'. This term attempts to capture the idea that the making of the apology, the putting on record of the victims' story or history is of value. This is because if the apology is endorsed by the state, presented in public with a degree of 'performativity' (see Chapter 1) it both affirms the story or history of the victims or those to whom the apology is made and challenges the narratives or conventional wisdoms that have marginalised or suppressed these stories or histories. This idea is expressed by Barkan who argues that 'at a very minimum … apologies lead to a reformulated historical understanding that itself is a form of restitution and become a factor in contemporary politics and humanitarian actions'.[1] One way to interpret Barkan is that a 'reformulated historical understanding' is a good in itself; what may lead from it is contingent.

There is some evidence that the public recording of itself may be important to groups; the idea that at least some of the 'truth' will out. This advantage of the 'recording' is often made in the context of marginalised groups such as indigenous peoples but also has a resonance with more specific injustices. The rhetoric of the Hillsborough campaigners, as indicated in banners of support, was that the apology had endorsed the truth and that the campaigners' narrative, their story, was vindicated. Leaving aside the debate about whether the historical truth can ever be established in a way post-modernists would contest, the public recording of stories and narratives of the wronged or victimised does challenge the existing 'truths'. Whether these are endorsed by the demos at large or lead to policy change or other forms of reparation is another question.

The second potential benefit of the apology can be subsumed under the terms 'acknowledgement' or 'recognition'. It may be objected that these terms cannot be used interchangeably; however in the literature on apology they capture similar if not identical ideas. For example, Govier and Verwoerd do not distinguish between the concepts: 'the power and importance of apology lie in its potential to offer victims a *moral recognition or acknowledgement* of their human worth and dignity'.[2] The fluidity between terms and lack of clear barriers is also indicated by the discussion of 'acknowledgement' in Marrus; elements of which are very similar to what is here termed 'recording'.[3]

Let us try to elaborate a little on these terms. Although very few of the texts on apology specifically discuss or even mention them, the ideas around the importance of acknowledgement or recognition draw implicitly on the work of Axel Honneth and particularly Charles Taylor.[4] Their work can be seen in the context of both the rise of 'identity politics' and a concern with recognition, or lack of it, by others being crucial in the construction of our identity and also in a revival of interest in the conceptualisation of the self found in the philosophy of Hegel and Herder. Taylor sets out the ideas thus. 'The thesis is that our identity is partly shaped by recognition or its absence, often by the *mis*recognition of others, and so a person or group of people can suffer real damage, real distortion, if the people or society around them mirror back a confining or demeaning or contemptible picture of themselves.'[5] There are two points to be stressed here. One is that the lack of recognition that was considered by Hegel in relation to the self is also, in Taylor, applicable to groups. According to Thompson, for Taylor one element of recognition is respect. This is due to all humans given their capacity for rational agency. In this way, respect reflects and is connected to a 'politics of universalism'. Esteem, as a concept, relates to the specific traits, qualities or abilities of a group and connects to the ideas of a 'politics of difference'.[6] In relation to the apology, and particularly in relation to those concerning ethnic groups or aboriginal peoples, the ideas of Taylor might be more applicable than those of Honneth. This is because for Honneth, the three constitutive parts of recognition; love, respect (manifested through legal rights) and esteem are conferred on or won by individuals rather than collectives; with esteem being related to an individual's achievements or accomplishments within a particular society or culture.

This brief summary should indicate how the identity of recognition has been applied to the apology. Typically, the groups who have been victims of injustice or discrimination may also suffer socio-economic disadvantage and political marginalisation; the importance of the idea of recognition is that it focuses upon the possibility or actuality of a collectively experienced negative psychic effect brought about by distorted identities. This is important because it offers a framework for those theorists and activists who wish to focus on how past injustice can resonate strongly in the present and at the level of the collective.

This does not mean, of course, that this way of thinking about identity and recognition cannot be critiqued, including by those broadly sympathetic to the idea of recognition politics. An example is the work of Fraser who has engaged with Honneth and others, arguing that the identity and cultural focus of much of the 'politics of recognition' has neglected the importance of institutional practices in reproducing the exclusion of groups and has failed to accord sufficient importance to the persisting material dimension of disadvantage and exclusion.[7] In Thompson's summary, Fraser argues that 'any account of social justice that focuses on cultural recognition to the neglect of economic redistribution will inevitably fail properly to understand the nature of injustice'.[8]

One more example from the literature on apology will illustrate the use of recognition. Although she does not make reference to Taylor or Honneth and 'recognition' does not appear in the index of the text, Melissa Nobles' discussion of national membership would seem to echo these ideas. She argues that apologies to indigenous peoples are aimed at altering national membership; this membership having three dimensions, the legal, the political and the affective.[9] The last relates to feelings of belonging and linkages within the political community and reflects similar concerns to those found in the politics of recognition.

The third potential benefit to the recipients is that of reassurance. An apology may explicitly contain an undertaking by the state not to act in an unjust or injurious manner again or this may be implicit in the apology. This is linked to the idea of forbearance which was discussed in Chapter 1. While there can be no guarantees, given the possibility of regime change or seismic cultural shifts, the acceptance of the injustice of past acts has the possibility of providing reassurance to the wronged group.

As indicated above, these three potential benefits may not be 'watertight' classifications and may shade into each other. The 'recording' of the injustice or the history of injustices may be a part of recognition though is not as thoroughgoing as that term would tend to imply and recognition, however conceptualised, may bring its own reassurance. If one group (within the same polity) recognises the intrinsic worth and dignity of another group, the latter is likely to be reassured that its position in the national community is secure. It is the restoring of dignity that gives the apology a role in reparative justice.[10]

The principal potential benefit of the apology for the victims of the injustice and the apologiser is that of reconciliation. According to Marrus: 'Judging by the frequency with which themes of reconciliation appear in apologies, this goal is widely embraced as one of the purposes of the exercise.'[11] Reconciliation is obviously of mutual benefit in as much as it improves relations between groups within a polity or improves relations between states; therefore it is a potential benefit in cases of both inter-state and intra-state apologies. What constitutes reconciliation in the context of any particular polity may be very varied and difficult to assess and this theme will be considered further in this chapter.

The third category of benefit, or potential benefit, is that which redounds to the state making the apology. Many authors have noted that the apology can have positive effects on the state issuing the apology. The most widely cited of these are variations on the theme that the apology is made to indicate the current moral or ethical condition of the state; to try to establish its moral credentials, and, implicitly or explicitly, to distance itself from the previous injustices and transgressions enacted. Depending on the context, the audience for this attempt to refashion its image is potentially groups within the state, another particular state or the international community.[12] The following examples provide a flavour of this and how commentators have articulated this theme. Brooks states: 'When the government makes a tender of apology, it is attempting to reclaim its humanity, its moral character, and its place in the community of civilised nations in the aftermath of the commission of an unspeakable inhuman injustice.'[13] Celermajer argues that apologising states are trying to establish their political-moral identity and that 'the identity of the apologizing nation seemed as much at issue as that of the group being recognised'.[14] Govier claims that 'in the end, acknowledgement has something of value for perpetrators too: it is the foundation of a more realistic identity and history, an articulation of relevant values, a basis for addressing feelings of guilt and shame, and a crucial support for sustainable reconciliation'.[15] Löwenheim's focus is specifically on requests for forgiveness rather than the apology itself; however as the phenomena are often related the point is relevant. 'When a state commits a gross wrong, its recognition and the legitimate status it seeks in the present are jeopardised and a request for forgiveness can help to improve its image (and status) by detaching it from its historical image as a transgressor.'[16]

To summarise this crudely, these ideas relate to the idea that states frequently want to be, or appear to be, 'good' and to distance themselves from their former 'bad' manifestations. Two subsidiary observations should be made here. One is that this can be viewed as analogous to elements of the interpersonal apology whereby the apologiser tries to distance him or herself from the transgression in which the transgressing self was not the 'real' self. The second is that this way of thinking about the state can help address the criticism of the apology called 'presentism'. Presentism holds that one cannot judge the past in light of contemporary moral standards and therefore, for example, policies and practices which were not viewed as unjust or immoral at the time should not be apologised for now. There are other ways to critique this position; however the idea that states can reflect upon and try to develop their moral sense may allow for a condemnation of past practices even if they were viewed differently by contemporaries.[17]

Lastly, the potential benefit of the apology can go beyond the parties directly involved; that is, those apologising and those to whom the apology is made. If the apology becomes common practice, it can have a role in developing new standards and norms in international politics and developments in international law. The 'knock on' effect of apologies might then make it easier for other unjustly treated groups to gain an apology or other forms of reparation and also influence the future behaviour of states in relation to the respecting of human rights.[18]

The above section has indicated the principal benefits which are claimed for the apology. These have been classified into four groups in relation to whom they affect and on whom they impact. In summary, some observations about the general themes that pervade the literature supporting the potential of the apology will be offered.

First, as indicated above, although the potential benefits may be separated for classification, conceptually, and in practice, they appear closely linked. The recording of the injustice may in itself act as a type of recognition, and recognition may in itself lead to reassurance and help reconciliation. Second, the consideration, interrogation and reassessment of the past which is involved in many apologies are closely linked to both current and future concerns. The texts are replete with quotations and aphorisms about how the past shapes contemporary relations and has the capacity to influence future ones. Thus, proponents of the apology tend to reject the charge that their pursuit is a 'backward looking' project and of little relevance because the intention of the apology is to improve current relations between groups or peoples and to offer the hope of a more harmonious and secure future.

Third, the potential benefits are to be found in both improved political and social structures and arrangements and in the improved psychological well-being of individuals and groups. Therefore, the language used in the texts draws on both what might be termed the lexicon of political science and political theory and that of psychology and psychotherapy. This in part reflects the discipline background of the contributors to the literature; however it is also more than this. Perhaps more than most other projects that can be termed 'political' in that they involve state action, the apology is bound up with terms and concepts, even if used loosely and sometimes metaphorically, that draw on psychology. Hence, terms such as 'catharsis', 'transformation', 'trauma', 'closure', 'moving on', 'healing' and 'identity' figure prominently in the literature.[19]

Fourth, it is frequently and readily acknowledged that the apology alone and of itself may be insufficient to bring about the desired transformations of recognition or reconciliation. This reinforces the point made in Chapter 1 that other forms of reparation ('other' in that apology can be a form of reparation) may be required to supplement the apology.

Having outlined in broad terms the claims that are made for the potential benefit of the apology, the next section will consider some of the arguments for questioning the value of the apology.

The (potential) disadvantages of the apology: why it is, or can be, bad

Opposition to the apology can have various roots and justifications and these may vary depending on the type of apology being considered. For example, popular opposition to the granting of an apology to a former wartime adversary may be based on the perception that the justness of the war means that apology for particular incidents carried out in its prosecution, however brutal in themselves, do not require an apology. The nuclear attacks on Hiroshima and Nagasaki and the bombing of Dresden in the Second World War serve as examples of these incidents.[20] Another popular and populist critique, often related to wartime episodes, is invoking a lack of reciprocity or, to put it more simply, 'we won't apologise because they haven't'. The fact that another party has not apologised for an injustice or wrongdoing does not seem a very compelling reason or moral basis for one's own refusal; as the old adage has it, 'two wrongs don't make a right'. However, at the level of popular responses to the apology this sentiment does seem to have some purchase.

In attempting to classify the basis of objections to the apology, it is useful to consider them in relation to three concepts; those of consequentialism, citizenship and nationalism.[21] In the section above, it was noted that one defence of the apology, or grounds to support it, was that it contributed to justice or was in itself just. This may be true and could be defended on deontological grounds; one should pursue justice. However, in practice the pursuit of justice can conflict with other desirable ends of political activity or goods that the state wishes to promote and could be critiqued on consequentialist grounds. To take a hypothetical example, the granting of an apology may conflict with the ends of social cohesion and security.[22] If the apology provokes a 'backlash' by the majority against the minority group receiving the apology, the negative effects may be twofold in that relations between the groups worsen, thus increasing social disharmony, and the security of the minority group may be jeopardised or made more fragile owing to the resentment of the majority group. This potential problem is more applicable to intra-state apologies and relations between members of the same polity; however it can resonate in the sphere of inter-state apologies. For example, there have been physical attacks on Japanese supporters of apologies to other countries by right-wing compatriots opposed to the idea of apology.[23]

Therefore, one can make an argument that the apology should be judged on its likely consequences. It must be emphasised here that this does not, of course, mean that the idea of the apology is intellectually incoherent or politically untenable. It is consistent to support the principle or coherence of the apology and to accept that there may be counter reasons to any particular apology being offered based on a consequentialist assessment of the likely outcome. One reason to draw attention to this is that it acts as a corrective to what may be termed a more idealistic or essentialist advocacy of the apology in which its role in justice is emphasised and the issue of other competing and desirable political goods are underemphasised. In 'actual' politics, and a position supported by a realist conception of political practice, governments will weigh the claims of the apology as justice against the potential disbenefits outlined above.

The second type of objection is of a different order in that its critique of the apology is not contingent or consequentialist but rather holds that the apology is incompatible with certain conceptualisations of citizenship. Or, to be more precise, this is a flaw found in certain types of apology. The type of apology that is the focus of this critique is one made by states to minority groups, usually those mobilised around a particular ethnic identity, within the same state. This critique is best understood as a response to the perceived problems of what are variously termed 'the politics of multiculturalism', 'identity politics' or 'the politics of difference'. The ideas and policies associated with these terms, of which the apology is one, run counter to two conceptualisations of citizenship; one which may be termed the liberal or republican and the other the nationalist. The subject of the critique and the concept of citizenship are massive areas, so an attempt will be made here to offer a brief outline. The liberal or republican view of citizenship tends to emphasise its civic, rather than ethno-national, nature and 'difference blind' aspects which often underpin policies such as the separation of church and state.[24] These ideas of citizenship are particularly associated with the republican traditions of France where, as Stevens notes, 'the rhetoric of republican values … resists attempts to map or define cultural diversity' and the USA.[25] The second type, here termed the national often, but not necessarily, has conservative elements and tends to emphasise patriotism or a shared national culture as the basis of citizenship and of civic cohesion. Although these are conceptually different, they can co-exist within the same polity. For example, the construction of an 'American identity' to counteract the possible centrifugal tendencies of a society composed of multiple ethnic groups and constructed through waves of immigration has elements of both a republican and national project. By contrast, in Britain, concepts of citizenship that emphasise national traditions, cultures and patriotism will often, implicitly or explicitly, endorse the status of the established church, the Protestant tradition or an Anglo-Saxon heritage that is clearly not 'difference blind' or republican in orientation.

What follows from this is that the apology to minority groups is considered wrong in that recognising or emphasising the particularistic identity of the group runs counter to a view of citizenship constructed either on republican equality and civic 'sameness' or one constructed on national values. It should be noted here that this could be termed a principled argument in that the principle of citizenship is being undermined or disregarded. However, there is often an empirical or consequentialist component to these critiques as well. Opponents to multiculturalism, 'the politics of difference' or the associated ideas outlined above often argue that the politics involved with these concepts and movements are incompatible with the concept of citizenship properly constituted and also produce, or risk producing, bad consequences in that polities become more fragmented, less cohesive and 'Balkanised'.[26] Augoustinos and LeCouteur argue that Howard's opposition to guilt and shame which he perceived to be associated with apology exploited the idea that such an apology would be divisive and undermine national unity.[27]

These arguments seem to be less than persuasive. If we look at particular examples where apologies have been demanded, such as to the indigenous people of Australia or African-Americans for slavery (and its legacy) it can be argued that the demands for an apology relate to the fact that historically those countries' conceptualisation and practice of citizenship did not include these groups. Therefore, it is the deficiency of citizenship as practically applied that gives rise to injustices that the apology may address. For example, despite the republican concept of citizenship which is ideologically powerful in the USA, the acronym WASP (White Anglo-Saxon Protestant) representing a privileged grouping indicates that in practice certain identities and cultures were valued or seen as more 'American' than others for long periods in the country's history.[28]

A third basis of opposition to the apology is that of nationalism, although as will be demonstrated its impact is diverse and varied. As Miller states: 'in acknowledging a national identity, I am also acknowledging that I owe special obligations to fellow members of my nation which I do not owe to other human beings'.[29] As Miller discusses at length this does not mean we have no obligations to non-nationals; however we might assume *prima facie* that national identity might inform attitudes to, and impact upon the issuing of, apologies.

It is a commonplace to note that nationalism, or national sentiment, takes many forms from the reactionary and racist to the relatively benign and liberal, so it is implausible to believe that all nations or people who have a national identity will respond to the apology in the same way. However, nationalism has important effects on the apology. One impact is at the level of popular sentiment. There is clear empirical evidence that certain apologies have been attacked or not endorsed by members of the nation-state which offered them because those members interpreted the apology as undermining or infringing their (positive) perception of their state.[30] As Chapter 6 illustrated, debates and contention over the way a country's history is recorded and remembered and debates over the image that is projected of the country are found in many contemporary states. To put it another way, apologies are often interpreted as the 'doing down' of one's country and resisted for this reason. Political leaders with strong nationalist sentiments may also share these feelings and, as Miller points out, because they have greater obligations to members of their own state than to members of others, this may justify the refusal of an apology. To express it as a rough equation, it may be felt that the recognition of an injustice done to other nationals weighs less in the balance than the defence of the integrity of one's own nation.

It needs to be emphasised here that these are generalisations and the impact of national sentiment on the apology will be varied and contingent and obviously it does not preclude all apologies; the simple point here is that nationalism may make an apology unlikely in particular circumstances or undermine the impact of one given.

There are three additional observations that need to be made about nationalism and the apology in general. First, the concern with the image of the nation held by particular nationalists can work in opposite directions and thus have very different implications for the apology. As already indicated, there is evidence that significant numbers of people in many nations are opposed to apologies, or to particular apologies, because they tarnish the image of the nation. The argument here is that the belief that one belongs to a 'good nation' is a powerful and pervasive one and if the apology challenges this perception and highlights the wrongs and unjust acts of the nation it may be opposed.

However, the opposite outcome is also potentially possible. If the apology is interpreted as reinforcing or re-establishing the 'good image' of the nation it may thus garner support. As was discussed in Chapter 6, this is one motivation found in inter-state apologies. It would need more detailed empirical work to identify precisely the variables that influence the degree of popular support for an apology to another country. However, these are likely to include the form of nationalism in any given country (e.g. liberal, multicultural, exclusionary, reactionary), the way in which nationalist sentiment is shaped by public intellectuals or mobilised by political actors, attitudes to the other state and the type or severity of the injustice. In respect of the last point, one reason why apologies by Germany for the Holocaust gained widespread support in that country was because the enormity of the injustice to be acknowledged outweighed the concern that its acknowledgement would be 'doing down' the country. The point to be made here is that national identity and sentiment can have radically different impacts on whether an apology is enacted or not.

Second, what may be called the 'nationalist objection' to the apology that is based on the objection that it 'does the country down' is an objection based on partiality and particularity. By this is meant that it is not an objection to the intellectual coherence of the apology or to the apology *per se* since nationalists holding this position would not object to an apology made to their nation since the 'doing down' would redound to the apologising nation to which they have no national attachment or sense of solidarity.

Third, if national identity or solidarity is an important factor in the apology it would seem to follow that apologies to co-nationals would be easier to make or win wider support than those to other countries and their citizens. It is not clear whether this is the case; however what is clear is that a sizeable minority of white Australians opposed an apology to indigenous Australians and a majority of white Americans have opposed an apology for slavery. Two factors may help to explain this. First, that although members of the same state, those groups may not have been identified or considered as co-nationals by those opposing the apology; there may have been a lack of affective connections. Second, the 'doing down of the nation' still resonates since the apology in these examples did or would make citizens confront the unpalatable aspects of the country's history that endorsed racism and systematic and institutionalised discrimination against members of the nation.

To conclude, the motivations and reasons for opposing the apology are varied. Some may be contingent and relate to the perception of the other party ('they won't apologise', 'their crimes were greater'). Others may be based on a consequentialist calculation that the apology will result in bad outcomes. A third category may be premised on the apology breaching conceptualisations of citizenship and a fourth relates to forms and articulations of nationalist sentiment. This does not mean all nationalists will oppose all apologies; rather that national identity or nationalist sentiment in particular conjunctures will make an apology appear ideologically or emotionally unpalatable.

The actual benefits of the apology

In the section at the beginning of this chapter the potential advantages and benefits of the apology which feature in much of the literature on the subject were addressed. This purpose of this section is to consider further whether these potential benefits translate into real or actual benefits.

Although there is much empirical work on apologies and particularly in relation to the form the apology takes and the context in which it is delivered, it is far from clear that the claimed potential benefits of the apology are often realised. There are two points to be emphasised here. First, the actual or realised benefits of the apology are, in principle, amenable to empirical investigation and detailed studies of the outcomes and impacts of particular apologies is an area that would repay further academic investigation. Second, however, an increase in such studies would not necessarily resolve these issues because of three specific difficulties in assessing the benefits or otherwise of particular apologies. This is not to argue that there are no yardsticks or criteria for assessment or that some apologies can be roughly judged more successful than others; rather it is a claim that there are some methodological difficulties in such assessments.

First, let us consider further two of the concepts that are frequently considered to be benefits, or potential benefits, of the apology; those of recognition and reconciliation (see first section above). More specifically, how can we assess whether these have occurred? Part of the problem here is that both of these terms, if not essentially contested concepts, have various meanings or can be conceptualised in various ways and some examples will help to demonstrate this. In relation to recognition, it is plausible that a public apology with the appropriate formality and solemnity or other aspects of the 'performativity' outlined in Chapter 1, might constitute recognition. Therefore, Prime Minister Rudd's apology to indigenous Australians in 2008 could be interpreted as recognising this group of people as one worthy of respect and full citizenship. However, another reading or interpretation of recognition may see this as a rather minimalist or attenuated conceptualisation and hold that recognition does, or should, encompass a more profound attitudinal or affective disposition of the dominant groups within society. So, for example, if the public apology takes place yet the majority group within a polity retains dismissive and contemptuous attitudes towards the minority group, it is reasonable to argue that recognition has not been realised. It would seem that the way that Honneth and Taylor conceive of recognition implies or entails that some attitudinal shift needs to occur at societal level and that public statements might or would not be sufficient to fulfil the criterion of recognition. It is interesting to note that Rudd himself alluded to this difficulty in a statement issued on the fourth anniversary of the apology in February 2012. He stated:

> Aboriginal people tell me there has been some healing of the soul for our First Australians over the last several years. They also tell me that they have a new-found sense of dignity, identity, and respect, in part because the attitude of non-indigenous Australians is changing. The truth is both of these are slow processes and intangibles such as these by definition ultimately defy measurement. But intangible does not mean unimportant. Because these deep questions of self-respect radically influence what we do, whether we are conscious of it or not.[31]

Rudd is quoted at length here because he articulates well the salient points. He goes on to detail what can be measured in terms of specific policy indicators (e.g. educational achievement, infant mortality) which links together three aspects of the apology that give cause for hope of progress in Australian society. One is the change of self-identity of the indigenous people, one is the change in attitude of the non-indigenous population and the third is the attempt at practical policy improvement. Although Rudd does not use the term 'recognition', the first two elements here fit well with the concept. This links back to the earlier discussion (see Chapter 1) of the significance of 'follow-up' to the apology as Rudd emphasises the importance of both policy change which can be measured and evaluated and the attitudinal shifts which will inform the policy change.

Northern Ireland will be offered as another example to try to illustrate the difficulty of 'pinning down' the concept of recognition. In the context of trying to bring an end to the Troubles there have been policy changes in many areas over a forty-year period and at least qualified apologies from some of the protagonists including the IRA and the British government. Various indicators, in particular the establishment of 'powersharing' political arrangements and the near cessation of political violence, could be adduced as evidence that the situation is much improved or even that the Troubles have ended. However, it is less clear that recognition has been one of the outcomes, if by recognition is meant an endorsement of the worth and equality of the culture and identity of the 'other' expressed either by nationalists or unionists. Hypothetically, attitudes to the 'other' and their identity may move along the spectrum from overt hostility, mute contempt, indifference, grudging acceptance, toleration to positive endorsement and acknowledgement.[32] While opinion polls and surveys may provide some information, it remains the case that attitudinal and ideational shifts may be difficult to record accurately.[33] If this is true, it may caution against trying to claim too much for recognition as an outcome for the apology and also indicate that progress can be made even if recognition is attenuated, partial or remains elusive.

The second concept that would repay some more discussion is 'reconciliation'. A recurring theme of this text has been the importance of context or specificity in discussing the apology and clearly what might constitute reconciliation will vary from case to case and be related to the prior relationship between the groups involved. As Cochrane has pointed out, there is no simple definitional boundary to the concept of reconciliation.[34] The broad nature of reconciliation is also emphasised by Ramsbotham, Woodhouse and Miall who identify four stages of reconciliation in relation to conflict resolution.[35] The first they describe as the stage of political closure where a return to violence is unlikely and a move to deeper processes of reconciliation can begin. The second stage is the process of overcoming polarisation and the 'rehumanising' of the other party. The third stage is marked by structural and institutional change often aimed at more inclusive political arrangements and fairer economic distribution. It is at the fourth stage which they call 'celebrating difference and reconciling former enemies' that forgiveness, acknowledgement and apology take place.[36] If their stages approach is correct, it means that the apology would typically occur at the end of a process of reconciliation rather than, as some of the apology literature suggests, be a producer or catalyst of reconciliation. That reconciliation can take place prior to an apology, and therefore without one, is borne out by Lind who argues that international reconciliation does not, certainly in all cases, require an apology as it often precedes the apology.[37]

A third example of the literature on reconciliation will be considered here. This text is a philosophical study and more extended than the two referenced above.[38] Murphy echoes Cochrane in arguing that there is no consensus about what constitutes reconciliation and her objective is to develop a more robust definition of political reconciliation.[39] Murphy's analysis is directed towards states that have been afflicted by civil conflict and are in the process of political transition. By implication, her analysis will not apply to more stable states where reconciliation needs to be less thoroughgoing.

Murphy is critical of formulations of reconciliation that try to apply concepts, such as forgiveness and trust, from the personal sphere to the arena of political reconciliation. Therefore, she tries to delineate the forms applicable to political reconciliation. To summarise her position, she argues that civil conflict and the accompanying violations undermine political reciprocity and respect for moral agency. In other words, such political systems flout legal procedures or use legal procedures and laws in unjust ways in favour of repressive groups. Moral agency is undermined by, among other factors, violence, sexual violence and lack of access to economic resources.

Political reconciliation thus has three inter-connected components. First, it needs to establish the rule and practice of law which all in society can respect. Second, it needs to develop political trust. This is distinguished from a looser or wider definition of trust since it is not an affective characteristic at the personal level but relates to political connections. 'Political trust is defined first by an attitude of optimism with respect to the competence and will of other citizens and officials. This attitude refers to a hopeful anticipation that citizens and officials will display the relevant competence and will in their interactions with others.'[40]

The third requirement is to address or repair the reduction in people's capabilities that occurs in civil conflict. Capability is defined as the 'effective freedom or genuine opportunity of individuals to achieve valuable doings and beings, or functionings.'[41] The concept relates to the idea that individuals as moral agents both need certain things or resources and have the opportunity to operationalise them to lead decent lives. Murphy considers that four particular capabilities are reduced or undermined by civil conflict that relate to a person's political relationships and their ability to function as a citizen. These are 'the capabilities of being respected, being recognised as a member of a political community, being an effective participant in the economic, social, and political life of the community; and fulfilling basic functionings that are necessary in order to survive and to escape poverty'.[42]

The main objective of Murphy is to fashion a theory of political reconciliation that pays due attention to the institutional, resource and attitudinal aspects and to provide a holistic account. An interesting aspect of this theory in relation to the theme of the apology is that the concept does not appear in the text and there are no bibliographical entries of material relating to it. The inference from this is that either Murphy believes the apology is irrelevant to the issue of political reconciliation or that the discipline of conflict resolution studies exists in a world that the apology has yet to permeate.

Having said this, it seems plausible in principle that the apology could play a role in two of the arenas which Murphy has identified in her theory; one is the building of political trust and the other is the rectifying of the damaged capabilities manifest in a lack of respect or the lack of recognition in being excluded from membership of a political community.

In summary then, the attempt here is to provide a corrective to what appear to be claims for the apology as a producer of recognition or reconciliation made without sufficient consideration or reflection of what these might look like 'on the ground' and to argue that more investigation is needed concerning the connection between potential and actual benefits. While recognition and reconciliation may not be subjective terms, their content and meaning are diffuse which may make it hard to identify whether they have been realised.

There are two other reasons why it is difficult to gauge whether an apology has led to recognition or reconciliation, or to assess the relationship of the apology (or lack of it) to these concepts. The first of these is common to many areas of public policy and relates to the timescale over which any judgement or evaluation is made. An apology may be a 'one-off' event or may be part of a much longer process of negotiated statements, partial apologies and other forms of reconciliatory measures. Examples of the latter type include the case of indigenous Australians, relations between Germany and its Second World War opponents, between Japan and Korea and between Britain and Ireland. In all these cases there have been long and often complex negotiations and discussions aimed at the improving of relations. Given the nature of 'process', at what stage could one identify recognition or reconciliation as being achieved or, conversely, having failed? This is difficult to judge and, relating to the previous discussion and the Rudd quotation, if recognition or reconciliation involves attitudinal or ideological shifts amongst people these are unlikely to be realised in the short-term. Therefore, evaluating whether the apology is of benefit (and of potential use as a model for other policy-makers and actors) is more difficult than in policy areas that can have quantifiable targets and specific timeframes (e.g. increasing the proportion of 18–21 year olds in higher education by date *x* or reducing hospital waiting lists by date *y*). In practice, reconciliation between groups within a polity or between states may involve a mixture of institutional and policy changes and a degree of attitudinal or cultural shifts and to identify an end to such processes at which an evaluation can be definitively made is difficult.

The second point is implicit in what has been outlined above. Because the apology often accompanies other types of reparation, policy change or reconciliatory measures it may be methodologically difficult to determine what role the apology played. In practice, there is no way, or no easy way, to isolate the impact of the apology on reconciliatory processes from other measures that accompany it. This reflects more general epistemological and methodological questions about evidence and causation in social science which impact upon our appraisal of the apology and its efficacy.

None of this should be taken to imply that evidence cannot be sought. At a very basic level, if a group states that it is satisfied with an apology as an indication of recognition of a past injustice or judge that it results from an attitudinal shift from a previously dismissive majority then this may be adduced as evidence of impact. Additionally, although attitudinal change may be harder to measure it is not beyond evaluation. An example from another area may help to illustrate this. In the discussion concerning two well-publicised cases of alleged racial abuse by players in English football in 2011–12, there was a consensus among commentators, pundits, players and supporters that there was much less overt racism among supporters than in the 1970s and 1980s. While not 'scientific', this would indicate that an attitudinal shift had occurred over a generation that made the use of overtly racist language socially unacceptable. Whether this also marked a decline in racist attitudes *per se* rather than a perception that they should not be vocalised is more difficult to tell.

The aim of this section was not to deny the potential benefits of the apology but rather to highlight that it seems more difficult to demonstrate its utility than is implied by some of its advocates.

The apology: the state and the demos

This section expands a little on some of the themes that have emerged in the previous section and have appeared, at least tangentially, in other parts of the book. It was noted in chapter two that states that make apologies are democracies. Therefore, the governments or heads of state making the apology are usually, in some sense, speaking for or on behalf of the people. However, the pluralistic nature of democracy makes it implausible that all citizens would support the idea of an apology. As already indicated, there are numerous potential grounds for opposition including a rejection of the conceptualisation of responsibility which underpins the apology, a nationalist view which see the apology as 'doing down the nation', a lack of empathy with the group to whom the apology is offered seeing them as 'special pleading' and a belief that the apology will lead to an undermining of a common sense of citizenship or national unity. In terms of practical politics, it may matter less if these objections are unfounded, incoherent or illiberal (though they may be none of these) than the fact that they exist. In existing, the state will have to reckon with them.

Empirically, there is, unsurprisingly, a varying degree of domestic public support for different apologies or for potential apologies. To cite a few examples, there is majority opposition to an apology for slavery in the USA, there has been considerable opposition to the series of apologies made by Japan and there was majority support for the apology to indigenous Australians made in 2008.[43] In other cases, the 'low level' nature of the apology meant that there was relatively little public engagement so that it is difficult to gauge attitudes.

Two questions arise from these observations. Is it a problem if the democratic state (or a particular state) favours an apology and many or most of the citizens of the state do not and what can be done about it? These issues will be addressed in turn.

It seems plausible that a 'gap' between the state support for an apology and the oppositional sentiments of the demos may particularly cause difficulties in the case of intra-state apologies. This is related to the ends and objectives of the apology discussed in the first section of this chapter. If the objective of the apology is to recognise the identity of a previously marginalised group and to try to extend to it the full affective dimensions of citizenship, this may need the positive endorsement of their fellow citizens rather than operate only at the level of elite policy-making. Relatedly, if the 'follow-up' to recognition or part of a process of reconciliation (a related objective) requires material resources for specific policies, this may be easier to obtain if the electorate or demos are supportive of the policy.

As always, there is the question of contingency here. The degree of public or democratic engagement or support for any particular apology needed to make it effective or meaningful will depend on various factors. However, it seems plausible to suggest that the more the demos as a whole endorse an apology the more it will satisfy those to whom it is made and the more likely it is that an electoral constituency which supports the related resource allocation can be developed or constructed.

If this is true, then a democratic state has two possible strategies by which to encourage support for the apology reflecting two strands of thinking about democratic practice and the connections between rulers and ruled.[44]

The first strategy is the dialogical in which the state can encourage dialogue and discussion and try to persuade the dissenters of the value and justness of the apology and to try to transform positions and sentiments. This is the kind of strategy alluded to by Mihai who argues that if liberal-democratic states are to try to 'live up to' their normative foundations of equal citizenship this may necessitate the making of apologies as 'exemplary political judgments'.[45] She who apologises for a community lacking consensus 'must convince the resisters that living up to the principles that define "us" as liberal democrats implies acknowledging wrongs done to specific groups among "us." "We" are the best that "we" can be when "we" look to our fundamental normative commitments and take responsibility for past suffering.'[46]

Political realists might object that the potential to garner support or change sentiments based on normative principles and liberal-democratic standards are difficult because a variety of attributes of some citizens including group loyalties, a lack of interest in justice or psychological resistance to reasoned arguments will undermine such efforts. If this is a plausible scenario, it is feasible that the state could attempt to mobilise support for the apology through appeals to other goods rather than justice or the normative potential of liberal democracy. This might also take the form of a dialogical discussion but one in which the benefits to the majority group in terms of social cohesion are stressed on the calculation that this is more likely to resonate with it. In practice, much public policy is enacted through both an appeal to normative values and the building of electoral blocs which are based, in part at least, on perceived self-interest. (For example, a normative end of social justice manifested through minimum standards of welfare provision may be secured through universal benefits since all of the electorate have a (self-)interest in supporting universalism.)

Either of these strategies seems plausible given that states typically have resources, financial and otherwise, which can be brought to bear on the changing of attitudes or behaviour of citizens. Therefore, if the state supports the apology it can attempt to persuade and cajole those of its citizens who do not by various means.

Alternatively, a second strategy could invoke the principles of representative democracy. These principles could resolve in principle the gap in attitudes between the state and the demos. If the citizenship does not have to be actively engaged in the promotion of the apology, and there is no necessity for affective or attitudinal changes, the state could pursue the apology in spite of the indifference or hostility of many citizens. If the apology is of low electoral salience, there may not be high domestic costs for its pursuit in such a situation. Representative democracy allows for and defends the right of representatives to make decisions and pursue policies that do not reflect majority opinion at any given time; reflection and the need for a longer-term perspective are often cited as reasons why this is efficacious.[47] That this principle is well established in the UK is illustrated by policies relating to, for example, terms of EU membership and capital punishment over recent decades in which the views of the electorate at any given time are at variance with the political elites.

These points have been highlighted because of the potential tensions that occur when a state supports an apology and many of its citizens do not. The strategy adopted by particular states, for example a dialogic engagement to change attitudes, an attempt at relative insulation from populist pressure through mechanisms of representative democracy or the abandonment of the apology will be influenced by factors including the perceived costs and benefits and the political and democratic culture of the state.

Notes

1 Barkan, *The Guilt of Nations*, p. xxviii.
2 Govier and Verwoerd, 'Taking wrongs seriously', p. 140, emphasis in original.
3 Marrus, 'Official apologies and the quest for historical justice', pp. 34–6.
4 A. Honneth, *The Struggle for Recognition: The Moral Grammar of Social Conflicts*, trans. J. Anderson (Cambridge: Polity Press, 1995); C. Taylor, 'The Politics of

Recognition', 25–73 in A. Gutmann (ed.), *Multiculturalism: Examining the Politics of Recognition* (Princeton, NJ: Princeton University Press, 1994).

5 C. Taylor, *Philosophical Arguments* (Cambridge, MA: Harvard University Press, 1995), p. 225, emphasis in original.

6 See S. Thompson, *The Political Theory of Recognition: A Critical Introduction* (Cambridge: Polity Press, 2006) for a comparative study of the work of Honneth, Taylor and Fraser.

7 See N. Fraser and A. Honneth, *Redistribution or Recognition?: A Political-Philosophical Exchange* (London: Verso, 2003) and N. Fraser, 'Rethinking recognition', *New Left Review*, 3 (2000), 107–20. For an extended discussion and critique of Taylor, see P. Markell, *Bound by Recognition* (Princeton, NJ: Princeton University Press, 2003).

8 Thompson, *The Political Theory of Recognition*, p. 105.

9 Nobles, *The Politics of Official Apologies*, pp. 32–9.

10 Thompson, 'Apology, Justice and Respect', p. 34. As the title indicates, Coicaud also sees the apology as related to justice. Coicaud, 'Apology; a small yet important part of justice'.

11 Marrus, 'Official apologies and the quest for historical justice', p. 37.

12 For the inter-state dimension see Chapter 6.

13 Brooks, 'The New Patriotism', p. 226.

14 Celermajer, *The Sins of the Nation*, p. 42.

15 Govier, *Forgiveness and Revenge*, p. 148.

16 Löwenheim, 'A haunted past', p. 545.

17 For a critique of 'presentism' see Govier and Verwoerd, 'Taking wrongs seriously', pp. 150–3.

18 See Marrus, 'Official apologies and the quest for historical justice' and Gibney and Roxstrom, 'The status of state apologies'.

19 Honneth's conceptualisation of 'recognition' clearly has political and psychological dimensions within it.

20 In 1991, President Bush refused to apologise for the use of the atomic bomb. See G. Dodds, 'Political Apologies: chronological list', http://reserve.mg2.org/apologies.htm, p. 3, accessed 30 October 2012. President Clinton, often seen as an apologiser *par excellence*, said that the USA owed Japan no apology for Hiroshima and Nakasaki (Dudden, *Troubled Apologies*, p. 128).

21 One may support the idea of the apology in principle but find particular ones problematic in relation to the four issues discussed in Chapter 3.

22 Political realists often stress security and stability as important political ends which may conflict with a politics based on more abstract principles of, for example, justice. See W. A. Galston, 'Realism in political theory', *European Journal of Political Theory*, 9:4 (2010), 385–411.

23 For more on Japanese apologies see Chapter 6.

24 However, Kymlicka has noted that historically many liberals supported the concept of group rights. See Kymlicka, *Multicultural Citizenship*, pp. 61–9.

25 A. Stevens, *Government and Politics of France* (Basingstoke: Palgrave Macmillan, 3rd edn, 2003), p. 3.

26 For example, see A. M. Schlesinger, *The Disuniting of America: Reflections on a Multicultural Society* (New York: Norton, 1993).

27 Augoustinos and Le Couteur, 'On Whether to Apologize to Indigenous Australians', p. 252. Dawson and Popoff claim that Horowitz, an American conservative, equates support for reparations with disloyalty to the nation ('Reparations: justice and greed in black and white', p. 57).
28 See C. W. Watson, *Multiculturalism* (Buckingham: Open University Press, 2000), pp. 36–43 for a critique of Schlesinger.
29 Miller, *On Nationality*, p. 49.
30 As Lind points out 'people always have a hard time acknowledging hard truths about their own country's wrongdoing.' (*The Peninsula*, 'Apologies in Northeast Asia – A Discussion with Dr. Jennifer Lind', http:blog.keia.org/2012/08/apologies-in-north-east-asia-a-discussion-with-dr-jenniferlind, p. 2, accessed 30 October 2012).
31 K. Rudd 'Fourth Anniversary of the National Apology to Indigenous Australians', http://foreignminister.gov.au/speeches/2012/kr_sp_120210.html, p. 4, accessed 12 October 2012.
32 The persistence of 'peace walls' and the continuance of 'low-level' sectarian rioting and violence indicates the degree of recognition is limited.
33 The annual 'Data Yearbook' section of the journal *Irish Political Studies* provides some information about perceptions of the state of community relations; although this may be a related topic it is not the same as measuring recognition.
34 F. Cochrane, *Ending Wars* (Cambridge: Polity Press, 2008), p. 207, n. 1.
35 This would not be applicable to all apologies, reflecting the contextual point made above.
36 O. Ramsbotham, T. Woodhouse and H. Miall, *Contemporary Conflict Resolution: The Prevention, Management and Transformation of Deadly Conflicts* (Cambridge: Polity Press, 2nd edn, 2005), pp. 231–45.
37 Lind, *Sorry States*, p. 3.
38 C. Murphy, *A Moral Theory of Political Reconciliation* (Cambridge: Cambridge University Press, 2010).
39 *Ibid.*, p. 7.
40 *Ibid.*, p. 77.
41 *Ibid.*, p. 94.
42 *Ibid.*, p. 95.
43 For the USA, see Torpey, 'Paying for the past?' and Dawson and Popoff, 'Reparations: justice and greed in black and white'. For Japan, see Lind, *Sorry States.* In relation to Australia, Augoustinos *et al.* argue that Rudd mobilised 'widespread public support' for his apology (Augoustinos *et al.*, 'Apologizing for historical injustice', p. 529) and one estimate was that 30 per cent of Australians supported Howard's opposition to the apology (BBC News 'Australia apology to Aborigines', 13 February 2008, http://news.bbc.co.uk/1/hi/7241965.stm, accessed 12 October 2012).
44 This is not to suggest there are not other ways to think about democracy; it is that these two are useful in this context.
45 Mihai, 'When the state says "sorry"'.
46 *Ibid.*, p. 16.
47 In Britain, these ideas are associated with the eighteenth-century politician and theorist Edmund Burke.

Conclusion

On reflecting on the phenomenon of the political apology, I would emphasise two areas in conclusion. First, the political apology is an intellectually defensible idea. There is meaning in states or nations giving an apology; continuities in national identity or state structure make it plausible and defensible for the representatives of states to apologise for events long past and, unlike the personal apology, the lack of an emotional engagement does not undermine the political apology. Second, the effectiveness of an apology may be very hard to measure and the effects are likely to be influenced by a host of contingent factors. It is this second area which would repay further investigation and it would be valuable if scholars developed more detailed, nuanced and longitudinal studies of the impact and effect of the apology in politics. The themes explored in Chapters 5 and 7 illustrated that defining what an apology is supposed to do and telling whether it has done it, or will do it, are difficult issues but there may be scope for further work in this area which could increase the quantitative and qualitative data about the way in which people understand, interpret and respond to the apology.

Despite some detailed case studies, much of the academic and popular writing about apology too easily assumes that it is a `good thing' contributing to justice, recognition or reconciliation or a `bad thing' that is symbolic of an age in which either cynicism reigns or a cheap emotionalism has dethroned rigour and reason as drivers in the political sphere. It might be better to consider the apology as likely to have a variable impact and being of variable utility depending on specific factors and contingencies. So, for example, researchers might need to consider more what people understand by the apology, how they conceive of its relationship to emotions, how reactions to it are informed by underlying ideological assumptions and how politicians and the people's representatives try to influence, or do not try to influence, attitudes toward the apology. It is conceivable that the apology may be a means to justice, reconciliation and also a cynical attempt to deflect responsibility from the more contemporary transgressions of politicians. What would be useful is to investigate more how they may serve good or bad ends in particular contexts and are used in particular ways. The definitional and normative discussions and debates that have taken place over a decade or so need to be supplemented by the fieldwork and 'on the ground' research which could take us further in adjudicating whether apologies make a difference and in what ways to relations between previously estranged or antagonistic groups within nations or between states in the international arena.

These tentative recommendations reflect what I see as a *via media*. If there is a large gap between the real, concrete impact of the apology and the claims of some of its more optimistic or idealistic advocates this may bring the practice of apology into disrepute and feed cynicism in politics. This is why it would be sensible to recognise the limitations of the apology (and to try to measure its effectiveness) while at the same time making a defence of its integrity. The fact that some groups have indicated that the apology has contributed to their sense that historical wrongs are not being ignored and that their worth as citizens is being recognised means that it should be defended as one possible strategy in efforts to uphold or extend liberal and democratic values.

Bibliographical note

There is, as far as I am aware, no complete list of political apologies. A list compiled by G. Dodds entitled 'Political apologies: chronological list' covers the period to 2002 and can be accessed at http://reserve.mg2.org/apologies.htm. The appendix to Nobles, *The Politics of Official Apologies* lists apologies up to mid-2005. There is a website link to various articles and research about apology administered by R. Howard-Hassmann at 'Political Apologies and Reparations', www.political-apologies.wlu.ca.

The following references provide further details concerning case studies mentioned in the text. Where short titles are used, the full reference is in the Bibliography.

Australia

Augoustinos and LeCouteur, 'On Whether to Apologise to Indigenous Australians'; Augoustinos *et al.*, 'Apologizing for historical injustice'; Barkan, *The Guilt of Nations;* Celermajer, 'The Apology in Australia'; Celermajer, *The Sins of the Nation;* K. Rudd, 'Fourth Anniversary of the National Apology to Indigenous Australians'.

Blair and Famine

Cunningham, 'Apologies in Irish politics: a commentary and critique'.

Bloody Sunday

D. Cameron, House of Commons Statement, Hansard, 6th series, vol. 511, cols 734–61, 15 June 2010; J. Campbell, *The Inside Story of the Bloody Sunday Justice Campaign* (Dublin: Liberties Press, 2012); B. Conway, *Commemoration and Bloody Sunday: Pathways of Memory* (Basingstoke: Palgrave Macmillan,

2010); D. Murray, *Bloody Sunday: Truth, Lies and the Saville Inquiry* (London: Biteback Books, 2012).

Canada

S. Harper, 'Prime Minister Stephen Harper's statement of apology', 11 June 2008, www.cbc.ca/news/canada/story/2008/06/11pm-statement.html, accessed 6 March 2013; James, 'Wrestling with the Past'; Nobles, *The Politics of Official Apologies.*

Chirac and France

Celermajer, *The Sins of the Nation;* Fette, 'Apologizing for Vichy in Contemporary France'; J. Fette, 'The Apology Moment: Vichy Memories in 1990s France', 259–85 in Barkan and Karn (eds), *Taking Wrongs Seriously.*

Clinton apologies

Cunningham, 'Mea Culpa (almost)'; Dawson and Popoff, 'Reparations: justice and greed in black and white'; Gibney and Roxstrom, 'The status of state apologies'; Negash, *Apologia Politica;* Smith, *I Was Wrong.*

Germany

Barkan, *The Guilt of Nations*; C. Goschler, 'Disputed victims: the West German Discourse on Restitution for the Victims of Nazism', 93–110 in Berg and Schaefer (eds), *Historical Justice in International Perspective*; Jones, 'Apology diplomacy: justice for all?'; Lind, *Sorry States*; Löwenheim, 'A haunted past'; Negash, *Apologia Politica*; Renner, '"I'm sorry for apologising"'.

Hillsborough

House of Commons. Hansard 6th Series, vol. 550, cols 283–306, 12 September 2012. House of Commons. Hansard 6th series, vol. 551, cols 719–804, 22 October 2012. 'The Report of the Hillsborough Independent Panel', HC581, The Stationery Office, London, 2012 (http://hillsborough.independent.gov.uk/repository/report/HIP-report); P. Scraton, *Hillsborough: The Truth* (Edinburgh: Mainstream, 2nd edn, 2009).

Japan

Barkan, *The Guilt of Nations*; Coicaud, 'Apology: a small yet important part of justice'; Cunningham, 'Prisoners of the Japanese and the politics of apology'; Dahl, 'Is Japan facing its past?'; Dudden, *Troubled Apologies*; Lind, *Sorry States: Apologies in International Politics*; Negash, *Apologia Politica*; Yamazaki, *Japanese Apologies for World War II.*

Japanese-American internees

Barkan, *The Guilt of Nations*, in Brooks (ed.), *When Sorry Isn't Enough*, Part 4 'Japanese Americans'; Weiner, *The Sins of the Parents*; Weyeneth, 'The power of apology and the process of historical reconciliation'.

Katyn

BBC, 'Russian parliament condemns Stalin for Katyn massacre', www.bbc.co.uk/news-europe-11845315, accessed 15 January 2013; A. M. Cienciala, N. S. Lebedeva and W. Materski (eds), *Katyn: A Crime without Punishment* (New Haven, CT: Yale University Press, 2007); A. Paul, *Katyn: Stalin's Massacre and the Triumph of Truth* (DeKalb, IL: Northern Illinois University Press, 2010); G. Sanford, *Katyn and the Soviet Massacre of 1940: Truth, Justice and Memory* (London: Routledge, 2005).

Serbia

BBC, 'Serbian MPs offer apology for Srebenica massacre', 31 March 2010, http:// news.bbc.co.uk/1/hi/world/europe8594625.stm, accessed 18 January 2013; Denti, 'Public apologies in the Western Balkans'; T. Judah, *The Serbs: History, Myth and the Destruction of Yugoslavia* (New Haven, CT: Yale University Press, 3rd edn, 2009); *New York Times*, 'Serbia's Honest Apology', http//nytimes.com/2010/04/02opinion/02/Judah.html, accessed 18 January 2013.

Slavery

Berg, 'Historical Continuity and Counterfactual History in the Debate over Reparations for Slavery', in Brooks (ed.), *When Sorry Isn't Enough*, Part 6 'Slavery'; Brooks, 'The New Patriotism and Apology for Slavery'; Dawson and Popoff, 'Reparations: justice and greed in black and white'; du Plessis, 'Historical injustice and international law: an exploratory discussion of reparation for slavery'; Fleming, 'When Sorry is Enough'; Pettigrove, 'Apology, reparations and the question of inherited guilt'; E. Posner and A. Vermeule, 'Reparations for slavery and other historical injustices', *Columbia Law Review*, 103:3 (2003), 689–747; Torpey, 'Paying for the past?'; Weyeneth, 'The power of apology and the process of historical reconciliation'.

'Tuskegee'

W. Clinton 'Remarks by the President in apology for study done in Tuskegee', 16 May 1997, http://clinton4.nura.gov/textonly./New/Remarks.Fri/19970516-898.html, accessed 18 June 2009; J. Jones, *Bad Blood: The Tuskegee Syphilis Experiment* (New York: Free Press, 1981); S. M. Reverby (ed.), *Tuskegee's*

Truths: Rethinking the Tuskegee Syphilis Study (Chapel Hill, NC: University of North Carolina Press, 2000).

Bibliography

Abdel-Nour, F. 'National responsibility', *Political Theory*, 31:5 (2003), 693–719.

Aiken, N. *Identity, Reconciliation and Transitional Justice: Overcoming Intractability in Divided Societies* (Abingdon: Routledge, 2013).

Aitkenhead, D. 'I was never about boo hoo hoo', www.guardian.co.uk/books/2008/jun/26/healthmindandbody.lifeandhealth, accessed 9 January 2013.

Alexander, J. C. 'On the Social Construction of Moral Universals: The "Holocaust" from War Crime to Trauma Drama', 196–263 in J. C. Alexander, R. Eyerman, B. Giesen, N. J. Smelser and P. Sztompka, *Cultural Trauma and Collective Identity* (Berkeley, CA: University of California Press, 2004).

Allen, N. and S. Birch, 'Political conduct and misconduct: probing public opinion', *Parliamentary Affairs*, 64:1 (2011), 61–81.

Anderson, B. *Imagined Communities: Reflections on the Origins and Spread of Nationalism* (London: Verso, 1993).

Andrews, M., C. Jewitt and N. Hunt (eds), *Lest We Forget: How we Remember the Dead* (Stroud: History Press, 2011).

Angus Reid, 'Australians back apologies for Stolen Generations', www.angus-reidglobal.com.polls/30819/australians-back-poll-for-stolen-generations, accessed 5 February 2013.

Angus Reid, 'Britons and Northern Irish welcome PM's apology for Bloody Sunday', www.angus-reidglobal.com/polls.../britons-and-northern-irish-welcome-p, accessed 29 November 2012.

Ashplant, T. G., G. Dawson and M. Roper (eds), *The Politics of War Memory and Commemoration* (London: Routledge, 2000).

Attwood, B. 'Settling Histories, Unsettling Pasts: Reconciliation and Historical Justice in a Settler Society', 217–38 in M. Berg and B. Schaefer (eds), *Historical Justice in International Perspective: How Societies are Trying to Right the Wrongs of the Past* (Cambridge: Cambridge University Press, 2009).

Augoustinos, M., B. Hastie and M. Wright, 'Apologizing for historical injustice: emotion, truth and identity in political discourse', *Discourse and Society*, 22:5 (2011), 507–31.

Augoustinos, M. and A. LeCouteur, 'On Whether to Apologise to Indigenous Australians: the Denial of White Guilt', 236–61 in N. R. Branscombe and B. Doosje (eds),

Collective Guilt: International Perspectives (Cambridge: Cambridge University Press, 2004).

Austin, J. L. *How To Do Things With Words* (Oxford: Clarendon Press, 1962).

Australian Broadcasting Corporation (ABC). 'What do you think about saying "Sorry"?', www.abc.net.au/unleashed/37092.html, accessed 8 February 2013.

Australian Indigenous HealthInfoNet, www.healthinfonet.ecu.edu/au/health-facts/aboriginal-population, accessed 13 March 2013.

Barkan, E. *The Guilt of Nations: Restitution and Negotiating Historical Injustices* (New York: Norton, 2000).

Barkan, E. and A. Karn, 'Group Apology as an Ethical Imperative', 3–30 in E. Barkan and A. Karn (eds), *Taking Wrongs Seriously: Apologies and Reconciliations* (Stanford, CA: Stanford University Press, 2006).

Barkan, E. and A. Karn (eds), *Taking Wrongs Seriously: Apologies and Reconciliations* (Stanford, CA: Stanford University Press, 2006).

BBC. 'Russian parliament condemns Stalin for Katyn massacre', www.bbc.co.uk/news-europe-11845315, accessed 15 January 2013.

BBC. 'Serbian MPs offer apology for Srebenica massacre', 31 March 2010, http://news.bbc.co.uk/1/hi/world/europe8594625.stm, accessed 18 January 2013.

BBC News. 'Australia apology to Aborigines', 13 February 2008, http://news.bbc.co.uk/1/hi/7241965.stm, accessed 12 October 2012.

BBC News Northern Ireland. 'Assembly motion calls for Irish government apology', 18 September 2012, www.bbc.co.uk/news/uk-northernireland-19631027, accessed 7 December 2012.

BBC News Northern Ireland. 'Bloody Sunday report published', 15 June 2010, www.bbc.co.uk/news/10322708, accessed 1 February 2013.

Bell, C., C. Campbell and F. Ní Aolain, 'Transitional Justice: (re)conceptualising the field', *International Journal of Law in Context*, 3:2 (2007), 81–8.

Berg, M. 'Historical Continuity and Counterfactual History in the Debate over Reparations for Slavery', 69–91 in M. Berg and B. Schaefer (eds), *Historical Justice in International Perspective: How Societies are Trying to Right the Wrongs of the Past* (Cambridge: Cambridge University Press, 2009).

Berg, M. and B. Schaefer (eds), *Historical Justice in International Perspective: How Societies are Trying to Right the Wrongs of the Past* (Cambridge: Cambridge University Press, 2009).

Bilali, R. and M. A. Ross, 'Remembering Intergroup Conflict', 123–35 in L. R. Tropp (ed.), *The Oxford Handbook of Intergroup Conflict* (Oxford: Oxford University Press, 2012).

Bilder, R. B. 'The Role of Apology in International Law', 13–30 in M. Gibney, R. Howard-Hassmann, J.-M. Coicaud and N. Steiner (eds), *The Age of Apology: Facing Up to the Past* (Philadelphia, PA: University of Pennsylvania Press, 2008).

Bourke, J. 'Introduction: "Remembering" War' (special issue on collective memory), *Journal of Contemporary History*, 39:4 (2004), 473–85.

Bradshaw, B. 'Nationalism and historical scholarship in modern Ireland', *Irish Historical Studies*, 26:104 (1989), 329–51.

Brennan, Z. 'A miserable liar? Angela's Ashes inspired a new literary genre – but was Frank McCourt REALLY telling the truth?', www.dailymail.co.uk/debate/article-1201062/A-miserable-liar-Angelas-Ashes-i, accessed 9 January 2013.

Brooks, R. L. (ed.), *When Sorry Isn't Enough: The Controversy over Apologies and Reparations for Human Injustice* (New York: New York University Press, 1999).

Brooks, R. L. 'The Age of Apology', 3–11 in Brooks (ed.), *When Sorry Isn't Enough.*

Brooks, R. L. 'Not even an Apology?', 309–14 in Brooks (ed.), *When Sorry Isn't Enough.*

Brooks, R. L. 'The New Patriotism and Apology for Slavery', 213–33 in E. Barkan and A. Karn (eds), *Taking Wrongs Seriously: Apologies and Reconciliations* (Stanford, CA: Stanford University Press, 2006).

Bruckner, P. *The Tyranny of Guilt: An Essay on Western Masochism* (Princeton, NJ: Princeton University Press, 2010).

Burnham, A. 'Handshakes, embraces, tears ... the week the healing started over Hillsborough', *Observer* (16 September 2012), p. 29.

Burridge, N. 'Perspectives on reconciliation and indigenous rights', *Cosmopolitan Civil Societies Journal*, 1:2 (2009), 111–28.

Buruma, I. *The Wages of Guilt: Memories of War in Germany and Japan* (London: Phoenix, 2002).

Cameron, D. House of Commons Statement, Hansard 6th series, vol. 511, cols 734–61, 15 June 2010.

Campbell, J. *The Inside Story of the Bloody Sunday Justice Campaign* (Dublin: Liberties Press, 2012).

Celermajer, D. 'The Apology in Australia: Re-covenanting the National Imaginary', 153–84 in E. Barkan and A. Karn (eds), *Taking Wrongs Seriously: Apologies and Reconciliations* (Stanford, CA: Stanford University Press, 2006).

Celermajer, D. *The Sins of the Nation and the Ritual of Apologies* (Cambridge: Cambridge University Press, 2009).

Checkel, J. T. 'The constructivist turn in International Relations theory', *World Politics*, 50:2 (1998), 324–48.

Cienciala, A. M., N. S. Lebedeva and W. Materski (eds), *Katyn: A Crime without Punishment* (New Haven, CT: Yale University Press, 2007).

Clinton, W. 'Remarks by the President in apology for study done in Tuskegee', 16 May 1997, http://clinton4nura.gov/textonly.New/Remarks.Fri.19970516-898.html, accessed 18 June 2009.

Cochrane, F. *Ending Wars* (Cambridge: Polity Press, 2008).

Cohen, S. *States of Denial: Knowing about Atrocities and Suffering* (Cambridge: Polity Press, 2001).

Coicaud, J.-M. 'Apology: a small yet important part of justice', *Japanese Journal of Political Science*, 10:1 (2009), 93–124.

Cole, T. 'Review article: Scales of memory, layers of memory: recent works on memories of the Second World War and the Holocaust', *Journal of Contemporary History*, 37:1 (2002), 129–38.

Conway, B. *Commemoration and Bloody Sunday: Pathways of Memory* (Basingstoke: Palgrave Macmillan, 2010).

Crossley, N. *Making Sense of Social Movements* (Buckingham: Open University Press, 2002).

Cubitt, G. *History and Memory* (Manchester: Manchester University Press, 2007).

Cunningham, M. 'Saying sorry: the politics of apology', *Political Quarterly*, 70:3 (1999), 285–93.

Cunningham, M. 'Apologies in Irish politics: a commentary and critique', *Contemporary British History*, 18:4 (2004), 80–92.

Cunningham, M. 'Prisoners of the Japanese and the politics of apology: a battle over history and memory', *Journal of Contemporary History*, 39:4 (2004), 561–74.

Cunningham, M. 'Mea Culpa (almost): Clinton, atrocity and the politics of apology', unpublished paper, 2005.

Cunningham, M. '"It wasn't us and we didn't benefit": the discourse of opposition to an apology by Britain for its role in the slave trade', *Political Quarterly*, 79:2 (2008), 252–9.

Cunningham, M. 'The ideological location of the apology', *Journal of Political Ideologies*, 16:1 (2011), 115–22.

Dahl, D. S. 'Is Japan Facing Its Past? The Case of Japan and Its Neighbors', 241–55 in M. Gibney, R. Howard-Hassmann, J.-M. Coicaud and N. Steiner (eds), *The Age of Apology: Facing Up to the Past* (Philadelphia, PA: University of Pennsylvania Press, 2008).

Dawson, M. and R. Popoff. 'Reparations: justice and greed in black and white', *Du Bois Review*, 1:1 (2004), 47–91.

Dejung, C. 'Review article: A past that refuses to pass: the commemoration of the Second World War and the Holocaust', *Journal of Contemporary History*, 43:4 (2008), 701–10.

Denti, D. 'Public apologies in the Western Balkans: the shadow of ambiguity', paper presented at 'The Ritual of Public Apology' workshop, UCSIA, Antwerp, March 2012, revised version August 2012.

Dickie, M. 'Former Japan PM to lead opposition', *Financial Times* (27 September 2012), p. 10.

Dodds, G. 'Political apologies: chronological list', http://reserve.mg2.org/apologies.htm, accessed 30 October 2012.

Douglas, W. 'Congress apology for slavery just proves it's hard to say sorry', www.mcclatchydc.com/2009/07/02/71194/congress-apology-for-slavery-just.html, accessed 8 March 2013.

Dudden, A. *Troubled Apologies among Japan, Korea and the United States* (New York: Columbia University Press, 2008).

du Plessis, M. 'Historical injustice and international law: an exploratory discussion of reparation for slavery', *Human Rights Quarterly*, 25:3 (2003), 624–59.

Eley, G. 'The past under erasure? History, memory and the contemporary', *Journal of Contemporary History*, 46:3 (2011), 555–73.

Elshtain, J. B. 'Politics and Forgiveness', 45–64 in N. Biggar (ed.), *Burying the Past: Making Peace and Doing Justice after Civil Conflict* (Washington, DC: Georgetown University Press, 2003).

Feagin J. R. and E. O' Brien, 'The Growing Movement for Reparations', 341–4 in R. L. Brooks (ed.), *When Sorry Isn't Enough: The Controversy over Apologies and Reparations for Human Injustice* (New York: New York University Press, 1999).

Fette, J. 'The Apology Moment: Vichy Memories in 1990s France', 259–85 in E. Barkan and A. Karn (eds), *Taking Wrongs Seriously: Apologies and Reconciliations* (Stanford, CA: Stanford University Press, 2006).

Fette, J. 'Apologizing for Vichy in Contemporary France', 135–63 in M. Berg and B. Schaefer (eds), *Historical Justice in International Perspective: How Societies are Trying to Right the Wrongs of the Past* (Cambridge: Cambridge University Press, 2009).

Fleming, E. B. 'When Sorry is Enough: the Possibility of a National Apology for Slavery', 95–108 in M. Gibney, R. Howard-Hassmann, J.-M. Coicaud and N. Steiner (eds), *The Age of Apology: Facing Up to the Past* (Philadelphia, PA: University of Pennsylvania Press, 2008).

Fox, R. 'Disgruntled, disillusioned and disengaged: public attitudes to politics in Britain today', *Parliamentary Affairs*, 65:4 (2012), 877–87.

Fraser, N. 'Rethinking recognition', *New Left Review*, 3 (2000), 107–20.

Fraser, N. and A. Honneth, *Redistribution or Recognition?: A Political-Philosophical Exchange* (London: Verso, 2003).

Freeden, M. *Ideologies and Political Theory: A Conceptual Approach* (Oxford: Clarendon Press, 1996).

Freedland, J. 'A moment of madness?', *Guardian* (13 August 2007), www.guardian.co.uk/uk/2007/aug/13britishidentity.monarchy, accessed 9 October 2012.

Furedi, F. *Therapy Culture: Cultivating Vulnerability in an Uncertain Age* (London: Routledge, 2004).

Galston, W. A. 'Realism in political theory', *European Journal of Political Theory*, 9:4 (2010), 385–411.

Ganesh, J. 'Politics should not be subject to the tyranny of the apology', *Financial Times* (21 September 2012), p. 9.

Gibney, M. and E. Roxstrom, 'The status of state apologies', *Human Rights Quarterly*, 23:4 (2001), 911–39.

Gibney, M., R. Howard-Hassmann, J.-M. Coicaud and N. Steiner (eds), *The Age of Apology: Facing Up to the Past* (Philadelphia, PA: University of Pennsylvania Press, 2008).

Gill, K. 'The moral functions of an apology', *The Philosophical Forum*, 31:1 (2000), 11–27.

Goebel, S. 'Review article: Beyond discourse? Bodies and memories of two World Wars', *Journal of Contemporary History*, 42:2 (2007), 377–85.

Goldwater, B. *With No Apologies: The Opinionated Political Memoirs of American Conservatism's Conscience* (New York: William Morrow, 1979).

Goschler, C. 'Disputed Victims: the West German Discourse on Restitution for the Victims of Nazism', 93–110 in M. Berg and B. Schaefer (eds), *Historical Justice in International Perspective: How Societies are Trying to Right the Wrongs of the Past* (Cambridge: Cambridge University Press, 2009).

Govier, T. *Forgiveness and Revenge* (London: Routledge, 2002).

Govier, T. and W. Verwoerd. 'Taking wrongs seriously: a qualified defence of public apologies', *Saskatchewan Law Review*, 65 (2002), 139–62.

Govier, T. and W. Verwoerd, 'The promise and pitfalls of apology', *Journal of Social Philosophy*, 33:1 (2002), 67–82.

Hague, R. and M. Harrop, *Comparative Government and Politics* (Basingstoke: Palgrave Macmillan, 8th edn, 2010).

Hamber, B. *Transforming Societies after Political Violence: Truth, Reconciliation and Mental Health* (London: Springer Dordrecht Heidelberg, 2009).

Harper, S. 'Prime Minister Stephen Harper's statement of apology', 11 June 2008, www.cbc.ca/news/canada/story/2008/06/11pm-statement.html, accessed 6 March 2013.

Harris, S., K. Grainger and L. Mullany, 'The pragmatics of political apologies', *Discourse and Society*, 17:6 (2006), 715–37.

Hastie, B. '"Excusing the inexcusable": justifying injustice in Nelson's Sorry speech', *Discourse and Society*, 20:6 (2009), 705–25.

Hayner, P. B. *Unspeakable Truths: Facing the Challenge of Truth Commissions* (London: Routledge, 2001).

Hayner, P. B. *Unspeakable Truths: Transitional Justice and the Challenge of Truth Commissions* (Abingdon: Routledge, 2nd edn, 2011).

Hazan, P. *Judging War, Judging History: Behind Truth and Reconciliation* (Stanford, CA: Stanford University Press, 2010).

Hislop, I. *Ian Hislop's Stiff Upper Lip – An Emotional History of Britain* (BBC 2: 2/9/16 October 2012).

Honneth, A. *The Struggle for Recognition: the Moral Grammar of Social Conflicts*, trans. J. Anderson (Cambridge: Polity Press, 1995).

Horelt, M.-A. 'Public dramas of reconciliation: the ethnographic study of ceremonial and corporal elements in the deliverance of public atonement rituals in Katyn and East Timor', paper given at ECPR Conference, Reykjavik, 2011.

Horowitz, D. *Uncivil Wars: The Controversy over Reparations for Slavery* (San Francisco: Encounter Books, 2002).

House of Commons. Hansard, 6th series, vol. 550, cols 283–306, 12 September 2012.

House of Commons. Hansard 6th series, vol. 551, cols 719–804, 22 October 2012.

Howard-Hassmann, R. 'Public Apologies and Reparations', www.political-apologies.wlu.ca, accessed 7 March 2013.

Human Rights and Equal Opportunity Commission. *Bringing Them Home: National Inquiry into the Separation of Aboriginal and Torres Strait Islander Children from their Families* (Canberra: Commonwealth of Australia, 1997).

James, M. 'Wrestling with the Past: Apologies, Quasi-Apologies, and Non-Apologies in Canada', 137–53 in M. Gibney, R. Howard-Hassmann, J.-M. Coicaud and N. Steiner (eds), *The Age of Apology: Facing Up to the Past* (Philadelphia, PA: University of Pennsylvania Press, 2008).

Jones, J. *Bad Blood: The Tuskegee Syphilis Experiment* (New York: Free Press, 1981).

Jones, S. 'Apology diplomacy: justice for all?', Discussion Papers in Diplomacy, Netherlands Institute of International Relations, 'Clingendael', 2011.

Joyce, R. 'Apologizing', *Public Affairs Quarterly*, 13:2 (1999), 159–73.

Judah, T. *The Serbs: History, Myth and the Destruction of Yugoslavia* (New Haven, CT: Yale University Press, 3rd edn, 2009).

Katzenstein, R. 'Introduction: Alternative Perspectives on National Security', 1–32 in R. Katzenstein (ed.), *The Culture of National Security: Norms and Identity in World Politics* (New York: Columbia University Press, 1996).

Kenny, M. 'Taking the temperature of the political elite 2: the professionals move in?', *Parliamentary Affairs*, 62:2 (2009), 335–44.

Kenny, M. 'Taking the temperature of the British political elite 3: when grubby is the order of the day …', *Parliamentary Affairs*, 62:3 (2009), 503–13.

Kymlicka, W. *Liberalism, Community and Culture* (Oxford: Oxford University Press, 1989).

Kymlicka, W. *Multicultural Citizenship: A Liberal Theory of Minority Rights* (Oxford: Clarendon Press, 1995).

Lazare, A. *On Apology* (Oxford: Oxford University Press, 2004).

Lind, J. *Sorry States: Apologies in International Politics* (Ithaca, NY: Cornell University Press, 2008).

'The Living Consequences: exploring the legacy of slavery and race in the United States', http;//living.jdewperry.com/2009/06/senator-harkin-introduces-apology-for-slavery-and-racism, accessed 8 February 2013.

Löfström, J. 'Historical apologies as acts of symbolic inclusion – and exclusion? Reflections on institutional apologies as politics of cultural citizenship', *Citizenship Studies*, 15:1 (2011), 93–108.

Löwenheim, N. 'A haunted past: requesting forgiveness for wrongdoing in International Relations', *Review of International Studies*, 35:3 (2009), 531–55.

McCurry, J. 'Outrage as MPs visit "shrine of war criminals"', *Guardian* (19 October 2012), p. 38.

MacIntyre, A. *After Virtue: A Study in Moral Theory* (London: Duckworth, 2nd edn, 1985).

MacLachlan, A. 'The state of "sorry": official apologies and their absence', *Journal of Human Rights*, 9:3 (2010), 373–85.

Markell, P. *Bound by Recognition* (Princeton, NJ: Princeton University Press, 2003).

Marrus, M. 'Official apologies and the quest for historical justice', Occasional Paper No. 111 (Munk Centre for International Studies, University of Toronto, 2006).

Mey, J. L. *Pragmatics: An Introduction* (Oxford: Blackwell 2nd edn, 2001).

Mihai, M. 'When the state says "sorry": state apologies as exemplary political judgments', *Journal of Political Philosophy*, April 2012, 1–21, doi: 10.1111/j.1467-9760.2012.00418.x.

Miller, D. *On Nationality* (Oxford: Oxford University Press, 1995).

Miller, D. *National Responsibility and Global Justice* (Oxford: Oxford University Press, 2007).

Mingst, K. A. and M. P. Karns, *The United Nations in the 21st Century* (Boulder, CO: Westview Press, 3rd edn, 2007).

Moriarty, C. 'Review article: The material culture of Great War remembrance', *Journal of Contemporary History*, 34:4 (1999), 653–62.

Mulhall, S. and A. Swift, *Liberals and Communitarians* (Oxford: Blackwell, 2nd edn, 1996).

Müller, J.-W. (ed.), *Memory and Power in Post-War Europe* (Cambridge: Cambridge University Press, 2002).

Murphy, C. *A Moral Theory of Political Reconciliation* (Cambridge: Cambridge University Press, 2010).

Murray, D. *Bloody Sunday: Truth, Lies and the Saville Inquiry* (London: Biteback Books, 2012).

Negash, G. *Apologia Politica: States and their Apologies by Proxy* (Lanham, MD: Lexington, 2006).

New York Times, 'Serbia's Honest Apology', http://nytimes.com/2010/04/02opinion/02/Judah.html, accessed 18 January 2013.

Nobles, M. *The Politics of Official Apologies* (Cambridge: Cambridge University Press, 2008).

Olick, J. K. *The Politics of Regret: On Collective Memory and Historical Responsibility* (Abingdon: Routledge, 2007).

Olick, J. K. (ed.), *States of Memory: Continuities, Conflicts and Transformations in National Retrospection* (Durham, NC: Duke University Press, 2003).

O'Neill, B. 'Misery lit … read on', http://news.bbc.co.uk/1/hi/magazine/6563529.stm, accessed 9 January 2013.

Parker G. and A. Kazmin, 'Wreath for Amritsar carries message home to voters', *Financial Times* (20 February 2013), p. 2.

Paul, A. *Katyn: Stalin's Massacre and the Triumph of Truth* (DeKalb, IL: Northern Illinois University Press, 2010).

The Peninsula. 'Apologies in Northeast Asia – A Discussion with Dr. Jennifer Lind', http:blog:keia.org/2012/08-apologies-in-northeast-asia-a-discussion-with-dr-jennifer-lind, accessed 30 October 2012.

Pettigrove, G. 'Apology, reparations and the question of inherited guilt', *Public Affairs Quarterly*, 17:4 (2003), 319–48.

Posner, E. and A. Vermeule, 'Reparations for slavery and other historical injustices', *Columbia Law Review*, 103:3 (2003), 689–747.

Radstone, S. and B. Schwarz (eds), *Memory: Histories, Theories, Debates* (New York: Fordham University Press, 2010).

Ramsbotham, O., T. Woodhouse and H. Miall, *Contemporary Conflict Resolution: The Prevention, Management and Transformation of Deadly Conflicts* (Cambridge: Polity Press, 2nd edn, 2005).

Rayner, J. *The Apologist* (London: Atlantic Books, 2004).

Renner, J. '"I'm sorry for apologising": Czech and German apologies and their perlocutionary effects', *Review of International Studies*, 37:4 (2011), 1579–97.

Renteln, A. D. 'Apologies: A Cross-cultural Analysis', 61–76 in M. Gibney, R. Howard-Hassmann, J.-M. Coicaud and N. Steiner (eds), *The Age of Apology: Facing Up to the Past* (Philadelphia, PA: University of Pennsylvania Press, 2008).

'The Report of the Hillsborough Independent Panel', HC581, The Stationery Office, London, 2012, http://hillsborough.independent.gov.uk/repository/report/HIP-report, accessed 10 October 2012.

Reus-Smit, C. 'Constructivism', 212–36 in S. Burchill, A. Linklater, R. Devetak, J. Donnelly, T. Nardin, M. Paterson, C. Reus-Smit and J. True, *Theories of International Relations* (Basingstoke: Palgrave Macmillan, 4th edn, 2009).

Reverby, S. M. (ed.) *Tuskegee's Truths: Rethinking the Tuskegee Syphilis Study* (Chapel Hill, NC: University of North Carolina Press, 2000).

Riddell, P. 'In defence of politicians: in spite of themselves', *Parliamentary Affairs*, 63:3 (2010), 545–57.

Romney, M. *No Apology: The Case for American Greatness* (New York: St Martin's Press, 2010).

Rudd, K. 'Fourth Anniversary of the National Apology to Indigenous Australians', http://foreignminister.gov.au/speeches/2012 kr_sp_120210.html, accessed 12 October 2012.

Sandel, M. *Justice: What's the Right Thing To Do?* (London: Penguin, 2010).

Sanford, G. *Katyn and the Soviet Massacre of 1940: Truth, Justice and Memory* (London: Routledge, 2005).

Schlesinger, A. M. *The Disuniting of America: Reflections on a Multicultural Society* (New York: Norton, 1993).

Schmitter, P. 'Re-presenting representation' (Review article), *Government and Opposition*, 44:4 (2009), 476–90.

Schwarzmantel, J. *The Age of Ideology: Political Ideologies from the American Revolution to Postmodern Times* (Basingstoke: Macmillan, 1998).

Scraton, P. *Hillsborough: The Truth* (Edinburgh: Mainstream, 2nd edn, 2009).

Searle, J. *Speech Acts: An Essay in the Philosophy of Language* (Cambridge: Cambridge University Press, 1969).

'Senate Apology for Slavery Gets Mixed Reaction', www.npr.org/templates/story/story.php?storyId=105850676, accessed 8 February 2013.

Sher, G. 'Ancient wrongs and modern rights', *Philosophy and Public Affairs*, 10:1 (1981), 3–17.

Sher, G. 'Transgenerational compensation', *Philosophy and Public Affairs*, 33:2 (2005), 181–200.

'Slavery-Reparations', http://law.jrank.org/pages/10314/slavery-REPARATIONS.html, accessed 11 March 2013.

Smith, N. *I Was Wrong: The Meanings of Apologies* (Cambridge: Cambridge University Press, 2008).

Smith, P. 'Rudd apology draws measured praise', *Financial Times* (13 February 2008), p. 8.

Smith, T. 'The letter, the spirit, and the future: Rudd's apology to Australia's indigenous people', www.australianreview.net/digest/2008/03/smith.html, accessed 12 October 2012.

Sparrow, A. 'Politics Live with Andrew Sparrow. Bloody Sunday: the Saville report as it happened', www.guardian.co.uk/news/blog/2010/jun/15/bloodysunday-northernireland, accessed 1 February 2013.

Stevens, A. *Government and Politics of France* (Basingstoke: Palgrave Macmillan, 3rd edn, 2003).

Tavuchis, N. *Mea Culpa: A Sociology of Apology and Reconciliation* (Stanford, CA: Stanford University Press, 1991).

Taylor, C. 'The Politics of Recognition', 25–73 in A. Gutmann (ed.), *Multiculturalism: Examining the Politics of Recognition* (Princeton, NJ: Princeton University Press, 1994).

Taylor, C. *Philosophical Arguments* (Cambridge, MA: Harvard University Press, 1995).

Teitel, R. *Transitional Justice* (Oxford: Oxford University Press, 2000).

Thaler, M. 'Just pretending: political apologies for historical injustice and vice's tribute to virtue', *Critical Review of International Social and Political Philosophy*, 15:3 (2012), 259–78.

Thompson, J. *Taking Responsibility for the Past: Reparation and Historical Injustice* (Cambridge: Polity Press, 2002).

Thompson, J. 'Apology, Justice and Respect: A Critical Defense of Political Apology', 31–44 in M. Gibney, R. Howard-Hassmann, J.-M. Coicaud and N. Steiner (eds), *The Age of Apology: Facing Up to the Past* (Philadelphia, PA: University of Pennsylvania Press, 2008).

Thompson, S. *The Political Theory of Recognition: A Critical Introduction* (Cambridge: Polity Press, 2006).

The Times. Editorial: 'An Appropriate Apology' (21 February 2013), p. 2.

Torpey, J. 'Making whole what has been smashed: reflections on reparations', *Journal of Modern History*, 73:2 (2001), 333–58.

Torpey, J. 'Paying for the past?: The movement for reparations for African-Americans', *Journal of Human Rights*, 3:2 (2004), 171–87.

Torpey, J. *Making Whole What Has Been Smashed: On Reparation Politics* (Cambridge, MA: Harvard University Press, 2006).

Torpey, J. 'An Avalanche of History: The "Collapse of the Future" and the Rise of Reparations Politics', 21–38 in M. Berg and B. Schaefer (eds), *Historical Justice in International Perspective: How Societies are Trying to Right the Wrongs of the Past* (Cambridge: Cambridge University Press, 2009).

Tropp L. R. (ed.) *The Oxford Handbook of Intergroup Conflict* (Oxford: Oxford University Press, 2012).

Trouillot, M.-R. 'Abortive rituals: historical apologies in the global era', *Interventions*, 2:2 (2000), 171–86.

United States Department of Commerce. United States Census Bureau, www.quickfacts.census.gov/qfd.states00000.html, accessed 13 March 2013.

Vincent, A. *Modern Political Ideologies* (Oxford: Blackwell, 2nd edn, 1995).

Waldron, J. 'Superseding historic injustice', *Ethics*, 103:1 (1992), 4–28.

Watson, C. W. *Multiculturalism* (Buckingham: Open University Press, 2000).

Watt, N. 'Cameron to pay respects to victims of Amritsar massacre', *Guardian* (20 February 2013), p. 6.

Weiner, B. *Sins of the Parents: The Politics of National Apologies in the United States* (Philadelphia, PA: Temple University Press, 2005).

Wenger, K. D. 'Apology lite: truths, doubts and reconciliations in the Senate's guarded apology for slavery', *CONNtemplations, Connecticut Law Review*, 42:1 (2009), 1–11.

West, E. 'Mis lit: is this the end for the misery memoir?', www.telegraph.co.uk/features/3635834/Mis-lit-Is-this-the-end-for-the-misery-memoir.html, accessed 9 January 2013.

Weyeneth, R. R. 'The power of apology and the process of historical reconciliation', *The Public Historian*, 23:3 (2001), 9–38.

Yamazaki, J. W. *Japanese Apologies for World War II: A Rhetorical Study* (Abingdon: Routledge, 2006).

Index